# A BIBLICAL WALK THROUGH
# THE MASS

## UNDERSTANDING WHAT WE SAY AND DO IN THE LITURGY

Edward Sri

ASCENSION PRESS

West Chester, Pennsylvania

*Nihil obstat:*      Mr. William C. Beckman
                  Censor Deputatus
                  November 16, 2010

*Imprimatur:*      +Most Reverend Charles J. Chaput, O.F.M. Cap.
                  Archbishop of Denver
                  November 16, 2010

Scriptural quotations contained herein are from the Revised Standard Version–Catholic Edition (RSV–CE) of the Bible, copyright 1965, 1966 by the National Council of Churches of Christ in the United States. Used by permission.

Published by Ascension Press
Post Office Box 1990
West Chester, PA 19380
Orders: 1-800-376-0520
www.AscensionPress.com
www.BibleStudyforCatholics.com

Cover design: Devin Schadt

Printed in the United States of America
11 12 13 14 15 16 8 7 6 5 4 3 2

ISBN 978-1-935940-00-5

To my son Karl

# Contents

# Acknowledgments

I am grateful to my students at the Augustine Institute, Benedictine College, and FOCUS, with whom I have studied the Scriptures and the Mass in various settings over the past decade. Several insights gathered from our biblical journeys through the liturgy have found their way into the pages of this book. The staff at Ascension Press deserves many thanks for all their hard work on the various facets of this project. I am also thankful for Emmaus Road Publishing, who allowed me to explore some of these themes many years ago in a short piece for the *Catholic for a Reason* series. Curtis Mitch and Audree Heath offered some helpful feedback, for which I am appreciative. Most of all, I express gratitude to my wife, Elizabeth, whose patience and encouragement throughout this project—amid raising our children—has been a tremendous blessing.

## BIBLICAL ABBREVIATIONS

The following abbreviations are used for the various Scriptural verses cited throughout the book. (Note: CCC = *Catechism of the Catholic Church*.)

**Old Testament**

| | | | |
|---|---|---|---|
| Gn | Genesis | Jon | Jonah |
| Ex | Exodus | Mi | Micah |
| Lv | Leviticus | Na | Nahum |
| Nm | Numbers | Hb | Habakkuk |
| Dt | Deuteronomy | Zep | Zephaniah |
| Jos | Joshua | Hg | Haggai |
| Jgs | Judges | Zec | Zechariah |
| Ru | Ruth | Mal | Malachi |
| 1 Sam | 1 Samuel | | |
| 2 Sam | 2 Samuel | **New Testament** | |
| 1 Kgs | 1 Kings | Mt | Matthew |
| 2 Kgs | 2 Kings | Mk | Mark |
| 1 Chr | 1 Chronicles | Lk | Luke |
| 2 Chr | 2 Chronicles | Jn | John |
| Ezr | Ezra | Acts | Acts |
| Neh | Nehemiah | Rom | Romans |
| Tb | Tobit | 1 Cor | 1 Corinthians |
| Jdt | Judith | 2 Cor | 2 Corinthians |
| Est | Esther | Gal | Galatians |
| 1 Mc | 1 Maccabees | Eph | Ephesians |
| 2 Mc | 2 Maccabees | Phil | Philippians |
| Jb | Job | Col | Colossians |
| Ps | Psalms | 1 Thess | 1 Thessalonians |
| Prv | Proverbs | 2 Thess | 2 Thessalonians |
| Eccl | Ecclesiastes | 1 Tm | 1 Timothy |
| Sng | Song of Songs | 2 Tm | 2 Timothy |
| Wis | Wisdom | Ti | Titus |
| Sir | Sirach | Phlm | Philemon |
| Is | Isaiah | Heb | Hebrews |
| Jer | Jeremiah | Jas | James |
| Lam | Lamentations | 1 Pt | 1 Peter |
| Bar | Baruch | 2 Pt | 2 Peter |
| Ez | Ezekiel | 1 Jn | 1 John |
| Dn | Daniel | 2 Jn | 2 John |
| Hos | Hosea | 3 Jn | 3 John |
| Jl | Joel | Jude | Jude |
| Am | Amos | Rv | Revelation |
| Ob | Obadiah | | |

# INTRODUCTION

## *A 30,000-Foot View of the Mass*

I'll never forget a conversation I once had on a plane about the Mass. Sitting next to me was a middle-aged woman who was reading a Bible. Curious about her devotion to the Scriptures, I turned toward her and asked whether she was a Christian.

In a strong southern accent, she replied, "Yes, I'm a Pentecostal. Are *you* a Christian, too?"

I enthusiastically answered, "Yes, I'm a Catholic!"

To this, my new fundamentalist, Bible Christian friend replied only, "Hmmm."

I went on to ask her where she was traveling and learned that she was excited about going to North Carolina to visit her son. When she asked me about my destination, I once again gave a fervent reply:

"I'm traveling to a conference where hundreds of Catholics are gathering to study the Bible. In fact, I'm going to be giving a presentation on the biblical foundations of the Mass! I'm very excited. We're going to explore how all the prayers, signs, and rituals of the Mass are rooted in Scripture, and I hope to show that the more we know about the biblical roots of the liturgy, the more we will understand the beauty of the Mass and give ourselves more to Christ at every Mass."

"Hmmm...."

Unsure what to do with a Catholic who spoke passionately

about the Bible and the Mass, she proceeded to tell me about her own personal encounter with Catholic liturgy.

"I once attended a Mass with a friend of mine when I was eighteen," she began. "I had never been to anything like *that* before! Whew! There was a lot of standing up and sitting down and kneeling .... And people saying things from some book. I didn't know *what* was happening! But, ohhh yeass, I sure had a sense that there was something deeper going on there, in that there Mass."

Indeed, this woman was correct: There *is* "something deeper" going on in the Mass—something more than meets the eye. For some non-Catholics, like the woman on the plane, the Mass can be very confusing. With people standing, sitting, standing again, now kneeling, and periodically marking themselves with the sign of the cross, the way we worship in the Mass can, from an outsider's perspective, look like Catholic calisthenics. Moreover, the recitation of formulaic prayers and responses can seem to some to be a rather dry, mechanical way of talking to God. Worship should be much simpler and much more personal than all of this empty ritual and ceremony, some might say.

But even Catholics can miss the significance of what is really happening in the liturgy. For many people who grew up with the Mass, the prayers from the liturgy are quite familiar: "Lord, have mercy...Christ have mercy." "Lift up your hearts...We lift them up to the Lord." "The body of Christ...Amen." Many of us could recite these prayers from the Mass in our sleep. *But what do these words mean?* Do we really understand what we are saying when we address Jesus as "Lamb of God" or cry out "Holy, Holy, Holy Lord"? Or are we repeating things robotically every Sunday, unaware of the significance of these prayers and thus unable to give ourselves to God as fully as we could through them?

One key to unlocking the meaning of the rituals and prayers of the Mass is Scripture. As we will see in this book, the entire Mass is saturated with biblical references. The soul attuned to God's Word in Scripture cannot help but notice that the Bible calls out to us in practically every prayer, sign, and ritual of the Mass. Candles and incense, standing and kneeling, phrases such as "The Lord be with you," and "Glory to God in the highest"—all these have their roots in Sacred Scripture, whether it be a direct quotation or an echo of a biblical passage or a re-enactment of a biblical story or event. Knowing the biblical background of the prayers and rites of the Mass can shed much light on what is actually happening in the Liturgy. It will greatly enhance our participation in it, and thus enable us to enter more deeply into the mystery of the Mass.

Take, for example, the prayer "Glory to God in the highest," which echoes the angels' song over Bethlehem on the first Christmas. Just as the angelic hosts welcomed Jesus with this hymn some 2,000 years ago, so also do we prepare to welcome Our Lord on our altars in the Eucharist when we sing or recite this prayer at Sunday Mass. Similarly, when the celebrant washes his hands before the Eucharistic Prayer, this recalls a similar rite performed by the Old Testament priests before approaching God's presence in the sanctuary. When we see this ceremonial hand-washing at Mass, we should be in awe, since, from a biblical perspective, this signals that the priest is approaching the holy presence of God and will offer the most sacred of all sacrifices as Christ makes his sacrifice on the cross present in the Eucharist through the priest.

This book will take the reader on a biblical tour through the Mass, from the opening sign of the cross to the closing "Thanks be to God." In a sense, one could view this book as a "Bible study" on the Mass. Examining the main parts of the Mass through a biblical lens will give us a new perspective on the liturgy that we celebrate every Sunday. It will help us better realize the profundity of what is unfolding before us and grasp the meaning of what we are saying and doing as we participate in these mysteries.

This edition incorporates the new English translation of the Mass.[1] Although this book is about the Mass as a whole and does

---

[1]     All quotations from the Mass in this book are from the United States Conference of Catholic Bishops (USCCB) website (www.usccb.org).

not focus on the revised translation itself, it does comment on some of the more substantial changes, especially in light of their biblical background. The significance of this new translation should not be underestimated. Not only is it closer to the foundational Latin text of the Mass, and not only does it more beautifully reflect the language of Scripture; it also represents the biggest development in the Mass in the English-speaking world since Vatican II. People will need instruction in order to benefit fully from the revised prayers of the Liturgy. It is my hope that this occasion will provide pastors, catechists and parents with a unique opportunity to teach about the Mass, and that this book might be of service in those catechetical endeavors.

– *Edward Sri*
*Denver*
*October 1, 2010*
*Memorial of St. Thérèse of the Child Jesus*

# Part I

# Foundations

# What is the Mass?

From the time of the apostles, the Mass has been the central act of Christian worship. For the Mass is nothing less than the celebration of the Eucharist that Jesus instituted at the Last Supper, when he commanded his apostles, "Do this in memory of me" (see Lk 22:19).

All that happens in the Mass is difficult to summarize in a brief sentence or two, for the entire mystery of redemption is bound up with the Eucharistic liturgy. Indeed, as John Paul II writes, the saving mystery of Jesus' death and resurrection "is as it were gathered up, foreshadowed and 'concentrated' forever in the gift of the Eucharist."[2]

Here, we will briefly consider three aspects of the Eucharist that are foundational for our walk through the Mass: 1) the Eucharist as the memorial of Christ's sacrifice on the cross, 2) the Eucharist as the real presence of Jesus, and 3) the Eucharist as holy communion with Our Lord.

## The Mass as Sacrifice

The celebration of the Eucharist is often called "the holy sacrifice of the Mass." But in what sense is the Mass a *sacrifice*? This is, admittedly, not easy to see. After all, Catholics do not come to Mass like the ancient Jews went to their temple, bringing animals

---

[2]   John Paul II, *Eucharistia de Ecclesia*, no. 5.

to the sanctuary to be slayed, cut up, burned, and offered to God by a priest. The sacrifice taking place in the Mass is clearly not one of cattle, sheep, or goats. It does, however, involve a real sacrifice— the sacrifice of Jesus Christ, the Son of God, who in his death on the cross offered his life as a total gift to the Father and redeemed the world. According to Catholic teaching, the Mass does not merely recall or symbolize Jesus' death on the cross. It sacramentally *makes present* Christ's redeeming sacrifice on Calvary, so that its saving power may be more fully applied to our lives. As the *Catechism of the Catholic Church* teaches, "In the divine sacrifice which is celebrated in the Mass, the same Christ who offered himself once in a bloody manner on the altar of the cross is contained and offered in an unbloody manner."[3] A careful examination of Jesus' words at the Last Supper can shed light on this aspect of the Mass as a *sacrifice*.

On the night before he died, Jesus instituted the Eucharist as the memorial of his death and resurrection and a pledge of his love. In the context of the Passover, he took bread and wine and spoke of them, respectively, as his body being given up and his blood being poured out for the forgiveness of sins. He concluded the Last Supper by telling the apostles to celebrate this meal as a liturgical memorial: "Do this in memory of me."

One important point to note is how the language Jesus used when speaking about his body and blood had strong sacrificial overtones. He said his body would be offered up and his blood poured out. As we will see later, this language would have recalled the Jewish sacrificial rites in which an animal's body was offered up and its blood poured out in sacrifice. Thus, Jesus, at the Last Supper, was already anticipating his sacrifice on the cross when he referred to his body and blood being offered like a Passover lamb being sacrificed.

A second point is the Jewish notion of *memorial*. In Scripture, a *memorial* does not merely recall a past event. It makes that event present. Therefore, when Jesus said, "Do this in memory of me,"

---

[3]    CCC 1367; see also CCC 1362-72.

he was commanding the apostles to make present as a biblical memorial the sacrificial offering of his body and blood at the Last Supper. Indeed, the body and blood Jesus spoke of at the Last Supper is his body and blood that was sacrificed on Calvary, and this is what is made present to us in the Mass. As John Paul II explains, "Jesus did not simply state that what he was giving them to eat and drink was his body and blood; he also expressed its *sacrificial meaning* and made sacramentally present his sacrifice which would soon be offered on the Cross for the salvation of all."[4] Similarly, the *Catechism* teaches that the Mass "*re-presents* (makes present) the sacrifice of the cross."[5] Through the Eucharist, "the bloody sacrifice which he was to accomplish once for all on the cross would be re-presented, its memory perpetuated until the end of the world, and its salutary power be applied to the forgiveness of the sins we daily commit."[6]

## The Real Presence of Jesus

A second aspect of the Eucharist is that it contains the *real presence* of Jesus. The Catholic Church teaches that although Christ is present to his people in many ways—in the poor, in his word, in the sacraments, and in the prayer of two or more gathered in his name—he is uniquely present in the Eucharist. For in the Eucharist the body and blood, soul and divinity of Jesus Christ is substantially contained. Through the Eucharist, "Christ, God and man, makes himself wholly and entirely present."[7]

The Eucharist is not merely a symbol of Jesus. Nor is Christ only spiritually present in some vague way in the bread and wine. At the Last Supper, Jesus took bread and wine and said, "This is my body... This is the cup of my blood..." Unlike other Christian communities that view the Eucharist merely as a sacred symbol

---

[4]   John Paul II, *Ecclesia de Eucharistia*, no. 12.
[5]   CCC 1366 (emphasis in original).
[6]   Ibid.
[7]   CCC 1374.

or "reminder" of Jesus, the Catholic Church affirms that when
the priest at Mass recites these words of Jesus at the moment of
consecration, the bread and wine on the altar are changed into
Christ's body and blood. The theological term used to describe
this change is *transubstantiation*, which expresses how, by the
consecration of the bread and wine, "there takes place a change of
the whole substance of the bread into the substance of the body of
Christ our Lord and of the whole substance of the wine into the
substance of his blood."[8]

This change, however, is not a chemical one. All the outward,
sensible appearances of bread and wine remain. The host still
looks like bread, tastes like bread, and feels like bread. And the
chalice contains what to all the senses appears to be ordinary wine.
The chemical structures of bread and wine remain the same. But
underneath these appearances, Jesus' body and blood is really
present in the Eucharist.

When Jesus himself taught about the Eucharist, he used
language with a profound realism to describe how we will partake
of his body and blood. Not only did Jesus speak at the Last Supper
of the bread and wine being his body and blood ("This is my body...
This is my blood"), but when he gave his most extensive teaching
about the Eucharist, he said we must really *eat* his flesh and drink
his blood. So important was the partaking of his actual body and
blood in the Eucharist that he taught, "Truly, truly I say to you,
unless you eat the flesh of the Son of man and drink his blood you
have no life in you; he who eats my flesh and drinks my blood has
eternal life, and I will raise him up at the last day. For my flesh
is food indeed, and my blood is drink indeed. He who eats my
flesh and drinks my blood abides in me, and I in him" (Jn 6:53-
56). St. Cyril of Jerusalem, an early Christian theologian, exhorted
Christians to trust in Jesus' words about the Eucharist really being
his body and blood: "Do not see in the bread and wine merely

---

8    CCC 1376.

natural elements, because the Lord has expressly said that they are his body and his blood: faith assures you of this, though your senses suggest otherwise."[9]

## O Come, O Come, Emmanuel

One of the biblical titles for Jesus is "Emmanuel," which means "God with us" (Mt 1:23). Jesus is the divine Son of God who became flesh and dwelt among us. And he so desired to remain close to us that he gave us the gift of his sacramental presence in the Eucharist. He thus continues to be Emmanuel—God with us—in each and every Mass celebrated throughout the world. We should never take this gift for granted. The most amazing event in the universe takes place at every Mass: the Son of God himself comes upon our altars and dwells in our midst!

But God's desire to remain with us does not stop there. Christ's presence continues to abide in the Eucharistic species even outside of Mass for as long as the sacred species remain. This is why in every Catholic church the Eucharist is to be reserved in a sacred space called a tabernacle. We should reverence the presence of Christ in the Eucharist by genuflecting or making some other holy gesture as an expression of adoring Our Lord in the tabernacle. We also should try to spend time with Jesus in the Eucharist outside of Mass in the church or adoration chapel. This intimacy with Christ's presence in the Eucharist can bring great strength and consolation to the soul. St. Alphonsus Liguori notes how this is one of the most important practices we can perform: "Of all devotions, that of adoring Jesus in the Blessed Sacrament is the greatest after the sacraments, the one dearest to God and the one most helpful to us."[10] John Paul II taught that when we rest in the Lord's presence

---

[9]   As quoted by John Paul II in *Ecclesia de Eucharistia*, no. 15.
[10]  St. Alphonsus Liguori, *Visite al SS. Sacramento e a Maria Santissima*, Introduction: *Opere Ascetiche* (Avellino, Italy: 2000), p. 295. See CCC 1418.

in the Eucharist it is as if we become like the beloved disciple who rested on Jesus' breast at the Last Supper.

In all the tabernacles throughout the world, Jesus continues to be Emmanuel, God with us. There, in the Blessed Sacrament, we encounter the same Jesus who walked the streets of Palestine, healed the sick, called people to conversion, and offered them forgiveness of sins. And this Jesus continues his work of healing, forgiving, and redeeming in the world; only now he comes to meet us sacramentally in the Eucharist. Jesus longs for us to draw near to him, and he wants to do great works in our lives, just as he did for God's people 2,000 years ago. But we must come to him. And we must believe. John Paul II noted how Jesus longs for us to visit him in the Eucharist: "Jesus awaits us in this sacrament of love. Let us not refuse the time to go to meet him in adoration, in contemplation full of faith…Let our adoration never cease."[11]

### Holy Communion

The New Testament reveals Jesus to be the Passover lamb sacrificed on Calvary for our sins (see 1 Cor 5:7-8; 1 Pt 1:19; Rv 5:6). However, in the Passover, as in other Jewish sacrificial rites, it was not enough to have the animal killed. *Eating* the sacrificial lamb was an essential part of the Passover celebration (see Ex 12:8-12). A communion meal followed the sacrifice, and it was the shared meal that expressed the sealing of the covenant and forged communion between the participants and God.

This has important implications for understanding the Eucharist as *communion*. If Jesus is the new Passover lamb who was sacrificed for our sins, it would seem fitting that there would be a communion meal accompanying his sacrifice on the cross—a meal in which we would partake of the true sacrificial Lamb of God, Jesus Christ. Looking at it from a biblical perspective, we might almost expect

---

[11]    John Paul II, *Dominicae cenae*, no. 3; as cited in CCC 1380.

there to be a communion meal flowing from Christ's sacrifice. This would follow the biblical pattern of sacrifice and communion.

St. Paul points us in this direction in his first letter to the Corinthians, which reflects this Jewish notion of sacrifice and communion. He taught, "Christ, our paschal lamb, has been sacrificed. Let us, therefore, celebrate the festival" (1 Cor 5:7-8). Notice how Christ's sacrifice is understood to find its culmination in a festive meal. Paul later makes clear what festive meal he has in mind: the Eucharist. In chapter 11, he gives an account of Jesus instituting the Eucharist at the Last Supper, and in chapter 10, he describes the profound unity established through partaking of Christ's body and blood: "The cup of blessing which we bless, is it not a communion in the blood of Christ? The bread which we break, is it not a communion in the body of Christ? Because there is one bread, we who are many are one body, for we all partake of the one bread" (1 Cor 10:16-17).

It is no wonder that the Catholic Church has seen holy communion as the climax of Eucharistic worship. As the *Catechism* explains, "The celebration of the Eucharistic sacrifice is wholly directed toward the intimate union of the faithful with Christ through communion. To receive communion is to receive Christ himself who has offered himself for us."[12] Indeed, holy communion is the most profound union we can have with God this side of eternity. God comes to us sacramentally on our altars at Mass and remains present to us outside of Mass in the tabernacle. This alone is quite awe-inspiring! But God's desire to unite himself to us goes even further. In holy communion, Our Lord enters our bodies, joining himself to our souls in this most intimate union.

This is the time to give our fullest attention to the Lord, as he dwells within us after holy communion. When we come back to our seat at church, we should pour our heart out to the Lord—to love him, to thank him, to share our deepest needs and petitions with him. In these moments after communion, we become like Mary,

---

[12]  CCC 1382.

who carried the God-Man in her womb for nine months. What a mystery! Mary had her creator and savior in her womb! And yet, what happened in Mary also happens to some degree sacramentally within us, when we receive the body and blood of Our Lord.[13] We become living tabernacles, housing the presence of the God-man himself. This is not the time to be looking around to see what people are wearing. This is not the time to be thinking about the football game later that afternoon or developing a strategy for how to get out of the parking lot quickly. This is the time to rest with Our Lord who has so lovingly come to dwell within us.

Receiving holy communion regularly can have a tremendous impact on our lives.[14] It can help us overcome weakness and sin, guide us in our decisions, support us in our trials and sufferings, and enable us to grow in holiness. By nourishing ourselves with the Eucharistic body and blood of Christ, we are gradually transformed by his very life dwelling within us. In a sense, to use a modern expression, we become what we eat! That is a point St. Leo the Great once made: "Nothing else is aimed at in our partaking of the body and blood of Christ, than that we change into what we consume, and ever bear in spirit and flesh him in whom we have died, been buried, and have risen."[15]

In conclusion, we have seen the Mass as sacrifice, real presence, and holy communion. With this basic background, we are now prepared to begin our biblical walk through the parts of the Mass.

---

[13]   John Paul II, *Ecclesia de Eucharistia*, no. 55.

[14]   Catholics are required to participate in the Mass on Sundays and Holy Days of Obligation. Reception of holy communion is encouraged every Sunday and feast days, and even daily (CCC 1389). However, one must be in the state of grace in order to avoid receiving the Eucharist in an "unworthy manner" (see 1 Cor 11:27-29). "Anyone conscious of a grave sin must receive the sacrament of Reconciliation before coming to communion" (CCC 1385).

[15]   St. Leo the Great, *Sermo 63*, as translated in Matthias Scheeben, *The Mysteries of Christianity* (St. Louis: Herder and Herder, 1964), pp. 486-7.

# Part II

# THE INTRODUCTORY RITES

# 1. The Sign of the Cross

*Priest:* In the name of the Father and of the
Son and of the Holy Spirit.

The sign of the cross is not simply a way to *begin* praying. It is itself a powerful prayer that is meant to pour out tremendous blessings on our lives.

Whenever we make the sign of the cross—whether at Mass or in our private devotions—we enter a sacred tradition that goes back to the early centuries of Christianity, when this ritual was understood to be a source of divine power and protection. In making this sign, we invoke God's presence and invite him to bless us, assist us, and guard us from all harm. It is not surprising that the early Christians made the sign of the cross quite often, desiring to tap into the power that lay therein.

The theologian Tertullian (c. A.D. 160–225), for example, described the common practice of believers who marked themselves with the sign of the cross throughout the day:

> In all our travels and movements, in all our coming
> in and going out, in putting on our shoes, at the bath,
> at the table, in lighting our candles, in lying down, in

sitting down, whatever employment occupies us, we
mark our foreheads with the sign of the cross.[16]

Other early Christians saw the sign of the cross as demarcating
God's faithful people, helping souls fight temptation, protecting
them from all evil, and even bringing terror to the devils. St. John
Chrysostom (A.D. 347–407), for example, exhorted God's people
to turn constantly to the power of Christ found in the sign of the
cross:

> Never leave your house without making the sign of the
> cross. It will be to you a staff, a weapon, an impregnable
> fortress. Neither man nor demon will dare to attack
> you, seeing you covered with such powerful armor.
> Let this sign teach you that you are a soldier, ready to
> combat against the demons, and ready to fight for the
> crown of justice. Are you ignorant of what the cross has
> done? It has vanquished death, destroyed sin, emptied
> hell, dethroned Satan, and restored the universe. Would
> you then doubt its power?[17]

*What did these early Christians see that we so often miss?* Why
did they so eagerly make the sign of the cross at the crucial turns in
their daily lives, while we sometimes perform this ritual merely out
of routine and sometimes even take it for granted? This reflection
will explore the biblical roots of the sign of the cross. The better we
understand the meaning of this prayer, the better prepared we will
be to receive the spiritual treasures God has in store for us each time
we sign ourselves and say, "In the name of the Father, and of the
Son, and of the Holy Spirit," especially at the start of every Mass.

---

[16]   Tertullian, *De corona*, no. 30.
[17]   St. John Chrysostom, *Instructions to Catechumens*, 2, 5, in Andrew Arnold
       Lambding, The *Sacramentals of the Holy Catholic Church* (New York:
       Benzinger Brothers, 1892), p. 70.

**The Sign of Ezekiel**

There are two principal aspects of the sign of the cross: the actual tracing of the cross over our bodies, and the words we recite while doing this. Let us first consider the sign itself.

The ritual of making the sign of the cross has roots in Sacred Scripture. In particular, some Church Fathers saw the Christian practice of the sign of the cross prefigured in the Old Testament book of Ezekiel, where a mysterious mark on the forehead was used as a sign of *divine protection* and as a mark *distinguishing the righteous from the wicked.* Ezekiel had a vision of many leaders in Jerusalem worshiping the sun and other idols in the Temple of the Lord and filling the land with violence (Ez 8). Because of their infidelity to God's covenant, the city would be punished and the people taken into exile.

Not everyone in Jerusalem, however, went along with the wicked ways of the city. There were some who sighed and groaned over the abominations in Jerusalem and chose to remain faithful to God. These righteous ones would receive a mysterious mark: the Hebrew letter *tahv*—which had the shape of an X or a cross—would be placed on their foreheads. This spiritual mark was to set them apart from the rest of the corrupt culture and would serve as a sign of divine protection (Ez 9:4-6). Like the blood on the doorposts that protected Israelite families from God's punishment on Egypt at the first Passover, this mark on the foreheads in Ezekiel 9 would protect the faithful ones in Jerusalem when judgment fell on the city.

The New Testament saints are sealed with a similar mark. Drawing on imagery from Ezekiel, the book of Revelation depicts the saints in heaven as having a seal upon their foreheads (Rv 7:3). As in Ezekiel's time, this seal separates the righteous people of God from the wicked and protects them from the coming judgment (Rv 9:4).

It is not surprising that Christians have seen in the mark from Ezekiel a prefiguring of the sign of the cross. Just as the faithful people in Ezekiel's time were protected by a cross-like mark on their foreheads, so Christians are guarded by the cross of Christ traced over their bodies. And this signing has tremendous significance. From a biblical perspective, every time we trace the sign of the cross over our bodies, we are doing two things. First, we are expressing our desire to be set apart from the corrupt ways of the world in our own day. As in Ezekiel's time, there are many among God's people who do not want to go along with the empty ways of living prevalent in the world. In our own age, characterized by greed, selfishness, loneliness, troubled marriages, and disrupted family life, making the sign of the cross can express a firm commitment to live according to Christ's standards, not the world's. While the secular world holds up money, pleasure, power, and having fun as the essential marks of a good life, Christians pursue a higher path to true happiness, which is found only in the sacrificial love of Christ on Calvary—the love symbolized by the sign of the cross.

Second, when we sign ourselves with the cross, we are invoking God's protection for our lives. In the sign of the cross, we ask him to guard us from all harm and evil. Many Christians throughout the centuries have turned to the sign of the cross for strength to fight against temptation. Others have done so in order to seek God's help in the midst of suffering and great trials. Many parents trace the sign of the cross on their children's foreheads, asking the Lord to bless and protect them.

St. Cyril of Jerusalem noted these two dimensions of the sign of the cross—the distinguishing and the protective aspects—calling the ritual both "a badge of the faithful" and "a terror to the devils" who seek to harm us:

> Let the cross, as our seal, be boldly made with our fingers upon our brow and on all occasions; over the bread we eat, over the cups we drink; in our comings and in our goings; before sleep; on lying down and rising up; when we are on our way, and when we are still. It is a powerful safeguard...for it is a grace from

> God, a badge of the faithful, and a terror to the devils....
> For when they see the Cross, they are reminded of the
> Crucified; they fear him who has "smashed the heads
> of the dragons."[18]

We have seen how the ritual of signing ourselves with the cross has foundations in the Bible. Now let us consider the words we recite—words which also have deep roots in Scripture.

## The Power of God's Name

While signing ourselves, we call on God's name, saying, "In the name of the Father and of the Son and of the Holy Spirit." In Scripture, to call on the name of the Lord denotes worship and is often associated with prayer and sacrifice. It is an ancient practice found among the earliest followers of the Lord. Adam's son Seth and his descendants are described as calling on the name of the Lord (Gn 4:26). The great patriarch Abraham calls on the name of the Lord when he is erecting altars to God and consecrating the land promised to him (Gn 12:8; 13:4; see 21:33). His son Isaac calls on the Lord's name when he builds an altar at Beersheba (Gn 26:25).

In Scripture, a name is not merely a conventional way of referring to a particular person. A name mysteriously represents the essence of a person and carries the power of that person. Therefore, to call upon God's name is to invoke his presence and his power. This is why the ancient Israelites frequently called upon the name of the Lord, not only to praise him (Ps 148:13) and thank him (Ps 80:18; 105:1), but also to seek his help in their lives (Ps 54:1; 124:8). Similarly, whenever we call on God's name, we invoke his divine presence and ask his assistance with the various struggles we face each day. Like the Psalmist, we recognize that "Our help is in the *name* of the Lord, who made heaven and earth" (Ps 124:8).

---

[18] St. Cyril of Jerusalem, *Catechetical Lecture* 13, 36. As cited in Andreas Andreopoulos, *The Sign of the Cross: The Gesture, The Mystery, The History* (Brewster, MA: Paraclete Press, 2006).

This sheds much light on the sign of the cross at Mass. At the start of the liturgy, we invite God into our lives in a powerful way. We solemnly call on his name, invoking his divine presence and power. It is as if we are consecrating the next hour or so of our lives to the Lord and saying that everything we do in the Mass, we do in his name. All that we do—our thoughts, desires, prayers, and actions—we do not on our own, but "in the name of the Father, and of the Son, and of the Holy Spirit." Moreover, like the Israelites of old who invoked the divine name as they worshiped the Lord, we reverently call on God's name, asking for his help as we prepare to enter into the sacred mysteries of the Mass.

In the New Testament, Jesus' name is revealed to be on par with the holiness and power of God's name. St. Paul describes it as "the name which is above every name" (Phil 2:9). He says this name has power to bring all things into subjection to Christ: "At the name of Jesus, every knee should bow, in heaven and on earth and under the earth, and every tongue confess that Jesus Christ is Lord, to the glory of God the Father" (Phil 2:10-11). Other New Testament books make this point, too. In Jesus' name, the sick can be healed (Mk 16:17-18; Acts 3:6), sinners find mercy (Lk 24:47; Acts 10:43) and demons can be expelled (Lk 10:17). Jesus himself teaches that he responds to all who call on his name: "Whatever you ask in my name, I will do" (Jn 14:13; see also 15:16; 16:23, 26-27). Moreover, his followers who gather in his name will receive the blessing of his presence among them: "For where two or three are gathered in my name, there am I in the midst of them" (Mt 18:20). This is what we do at the start of every Mass: we gather in the name of God's Son. We invoke his presence among us as we confidently bring our needs and petitions before him.

## Making the Sign of the Cross Carefully

Yet in the sign of the cross we do not focus on the Son alone. We call upon the name of the Father, Son, and Holy Spirit, echoing

Jesus' great commission to the apostles: "Go therefore and make disciples of all nations, baptizing them in the name of the Father and of the Son and of the Holy Spirit" (Mt 28:19). These were the words spoken when we were baptized, when our souls were first filled with the divine life of the Holy Trinity. By repeating these words at the start of every Mass, we acknowledge the profound fact that we are approaching Almighty God in the liturgy, not because of our own merit, but by virtue of the supernatural life God graciously bestowed on us at our baptism. We come not merely in our own name, but in the name of the Triune God who dwells within us. We also are praying that this divine life within us might grow. In the sign of the cross, we pray that our whole lives may be lived in ever greater harmony with God—that all that we do, we may do in his name.

This is why we should make every sign of the cross with careful attention and reverence. Given all that this ritual means, we should avoid signing ourselves in a hurried, sloppy way. As Romano Guardini once wrote:

> When we cross ourselves, let it be with a real sign of the cross. Instead of a small cramped gesture that gives no notion of its meaning, let us make a large unhurried sign, from forehead to breast, from shoulder to shoulder, consciously feeling how it includes the whole of us, our thoughts, our attitudes, our body and soul, every part of us at once, how it consecrates and sanctifies us…Make a large cross, taking time thinking what you do. Let it take in your whole being—body, soul, mind, will, thoughts, feelings, your doing and not-doing—and by signing it with the cross strengthen and consecrate the whole in the strength of Christ, in the name of the triune God.[19]

---

[19]  Roman Guardini, *Sacred Signs* (St. Louis: Pio Decimo Press, 1955), p. 14.

## 2. Greeting: "The Lord be with you"

*Priest:* The Lord be with you
*People:* And with your spirit.

From a biblical perspective, "The Lord be with you" is no ordinary greeting. This is not at all like an exchange in which the priest says, "Good morning," and the people respond, "And good morning to you, too, Father!" If we truly understood the Scriptural background to these words, we might approach the liturgy with more fear and trembling.

On a basic level, these words convey the reality of Jesus' presence with the community of believers assembled in his name, for Jesus said that "when two or three are gathered in my name, there am I in their midst" (Mt 18:20). This liturgical greeting also expresses the profound reality of God's life dwelling within our souls by virtue of our baptism. With these words, the priest is praying that the divine life we received may continue to grow within us.

But the greeting "The Lord be with you" also recalls the words spoken to a whole roster of heroes from the Bible who were called by God to a daunting mission—a mission that stretched the individual beyond his "comfort zone" and forced him to rely on God as never before. And the future of God's people was dependent on how well this individual answered the call and played his part. Think of Isaac

(Gn 26:3, 24) and Jacob (Gn 28:13-15); Moses (Ex 3:12) and Joshua (Jos 1:5, 9); King David (2 Sam 7:3), the prophet Jeremiah (Jer 1:6-8), and the Blessed Virgin Mary (Lk 1:28). All of them heard this message at pivotal moments in their lives. On several occasions when God calls someone in this way, either he or his angels addresses the person with the assurance that "The Lord is with you."

Take, for example, Joshua. After Moses died, God called Joshua to the daunting task of leading the people into the Promised Land, where there were many large armies resisting their entry and many battles to be fought. Yet God told Joshua to be of good courage and to be confident that he would succeed because, "I will be with you":

> "No man shall be able to stand before you all the days of your life; as I was with Moses, so I will be with you; I will not fail you or forsake you. Be strong and of good courage; for you shall cause this people to inherit the land which I swore to their fathers to give them...Be strong and of good courage; be not frightened, neither be dismayed; for the Lord your God is with you wherever you go." (Jos 1:5-6, 9)

God called Gideon in a similar way. The book of Judges tells of how God sent an angel to Gideon to call him to rescue the people from the Midianites who had taken over the land of Israel. The angel greeted Gideon with the words, "The Lord is with you" (Jgs 6:12). Even though Gideon had no prior military experience and was from a weak clan and the least in his own family, God promised Gideon that he would lead Israel to victory over the Midianites— not because of Gideon's own strength or expertise, but because of God's presence with him: "I will be with you, and you shall smite the Midianites as one man" (Jgs 6:16).

Perhaps the best example is the call of Moses at the burning bush. In this famous scene, the Lord summoned Moses to a very difficult mission: go back to Egypt (the nation where people were trying to kill him; see Ex 2:15), confront the wicked Pharaoh who was enslaving the Hebrews, and convince him to let the people go.

Overwhelmed with the weight of what was being asked of him, Moses did not feel equal to the task. "Who am I that I should go to Pharaoh and bring the sons of Israel out of Egypt?" (Ex 3:11) Moses then does all that he can to get out of this God-given responsibility: He tells the Lord that people will ask him who this God is (Ex 3:13), that the people will not believe him and doubt that the Lord really appeared to him (Ex 4:1), and that he is not eloquent enough to be such a leader (Ex 4:10).

### Mission Impossible?

How does God respond to Moses' feelings of inadequacy as a leader? Notice that God does not send Moses to a Franklin Covey seminar to help him develop better leadership skills, or to a Toastmaster's conference to train him in public speaking. Rather, God gives Moses the one thing he needs the most: the assurance of his presence with Moses in this challenging mission. "I will be with you," God says (Ex 3:12; 4:12). Moses will fulfill his mission, not because of his own talent and skill, but because of God's help, which will enable him to accomplish much more than he ever could have done on his own. As St. Paul would say, God's power will be made manifest through Moses' weakness (see 2 Cor 12:9-10).

Do you ever feel stretched or overwhelmed with the demands of life? Do you ever feel like Moses—inadequate for the mission God has entrusted to you, whether it be in your marriage, in your family, in your work, or in living your Catholic faith? If so, the words at the beginning of the liturgy, "The Lord be with you," can both inspire and encourage you.

On one hand, from a Scriptural perspective, the words "The Lord be with you" remind us of the high calling we each have. As God's children, we each have a particular mission to fulfill in the Father's plan. When we hear these words, we should realize that we are standing in the footsteps of Joshua, Moses, Gideon, and many others who received a special calling from the Lord. We may not be called to defend God's people from pagan oppressors or to confront wicked dictators like Pharaoh, but each of us has a role that no one else can play—in our marriages, in our families, in our work, in our friendships, in our parish, and in our community.

On the other hand, these words also assure us that we have access to a higher power that can support us through the trials and challenges of life and help us be faithful in whatever task God has entrusted to us. If we feel uncertain or inadequate in parenting our children, in sharing our faith with others, or in a certain area of virtue, the liturgy reminds us that the Lord is with us to assist us. If we are facing a struggling marriage, a challenging situation at work, a battle with serious illness or the loss of a loved one, God is with us through these trials. If we are experiencing sorrow, discouragement, or darkness in our spiritual lives, the Mass reminds us that the Lord is truly with us, even though we may not sense his presence. But, most of all, this greeting points to the awesome realities in which we are all about to participate—the mysteries of Christ's death and resurrection and communion with Christ's body and blood. We are not worthy of so great an honor, but the priest's words remind us at the start of Mass that the Lord is with us. Just like Moses, Joshua, Gideon, and many others, we can confidently trust in the Lord's help. We can trust that God's strength will make up for whatever in us is lacking.

## Apostolic Greeting

Other ritual options for the opening greeting come from the words St. Paul used in his letters. For example, the priest may say, "Grace to you and peace from God our Father and the Lord Jesus Christ"—words that are derived from the initial greetings in Paul's epistles (see Rom 1:7; 1 Cor 1:3; Gal 1:3; Eph 1:2; Phil 1:2).

This line in particular underscores the fact that our faith comes to us from the apostles, to whom Christ entrusted his mission and authority, and who later passed that authority on to their successors. The bishops today are the direct successors of the apostles and share their apostolic mission with their priests. When we hear the salutation, "Grace to you and peace from God our Father and the Lord Jesus Christ," we become aware of our fellowship with the saints throughout the Church's history who have been greeted with these words ever since the time of St. Paul.

### "And With Your Spirit"

Finally, we will reflect on the new translation of our response to this greeting: "And with your spirit." This more adequately reflects the Latin text of the Mass and the language of St. Paul (Gal 6:18). Most of all, it brings out more fully an important theological point. In the previous translation, when we said "and also with you," we might get the impression that our response was merely intended to express a basic reciprocity: "May God be with you, too." But there is much more going on in this response. By saying "and with your spirit," the people are acknowledging the Holy Spirit's unique activity through the priest during the sacred liturgy by virtue of his ordination.[20] As Jeremy Driscoll explains, "The people are addressing the 'spirit' of the priest; that is, that deepest interior part of his being where he has been ordained precisely to lead the people in this sacred action. They are saying in effect, 'Be the priest for us now,' aware that there is only one priest, Christ Himself, and that this one who represents him now must be finely tuned to perform his sacred duties well."[21]

One modern saint once emphasized why such prayers for priests are important, especially in the context of the Mass: "I ask all

---

[20]   See Pius Parsch, *The Liturgy of the Mass* (St. Louis: B. Herder, 1957), p. 109.

[21]   Jeremy Driscoll, *What Happens at Mass* (Chicago: Liturgy Training Publications, 2005), p. 25.

Christians to pray earnestly for us priests that we learn to perform the holy sacrifice in a holy way. I ask you to show a deep love for the Holy Mass. In this way you will encourage us priests to celebrate it respectfully, with divine and human dignity: to keep clean the vestments and other things used for worship, to act devoutly, to avoid rushing."[22]

---

[22] St. Josemaria Escriva, *Christ is Passing By*, p. 15. As cited in Charles Belmonte, *Understanding the Mass* (Princeton, NJ: Scepter, 1989), p. 53.

# 3. I Confess ...

*"I confess to almighty God*
*and to you, my brothers and sisters,*
*that I have greatly sinned,*
*in my thoughts and in my words,*
*in what I have done and in what I have failed to do,*
*through my fault, through my fault,*
*through my most grievous fault;*
*therefore I ask blessed Mary ever-Virgin,*
*all the Angels and Saints,*
*and you, my brothers and sisters,*
*to pray for me to the Lord our God."*

Throughout the Old Testament, when God manifests his divine presence to his people, it is usually quite unexpected. They respond with a holy fear and awe, sometimes even throwing themselves on the ground or covering their faces, as they acknowledge their unworthiness to stand in his presence (Gn 17:2; 28:17; Ex 3:6; 19:16). A similar response is given by Peter, James, and John when they suddenly see Jesus' glory revealed at the transfiguration (Mt 17:6), and by John alone when he unexpectedly sees Christ in his glory during a heavenly vision (Rv 1:17).

However, when the people were given advance notice of God's coming among them, they took time to prepare carefully for this holy encounter. For example, at Mount Sinai, Israel had three days to get ready to meet the Lord, who would come to them in thunder, lightning, and cloud and speak the words of the covenant—the Ten Commandments—directly to the people. In those days of preparation, they were instructed to consecrate themselves to the Lord and to wash their garments (Ex 19:9–19).

We, too, are called to prepare ourselves for a sacred encounter with the Lord every time we go to Mass. Yet our meeting with God is more profound than anyone in ancient Israel ever imagined. For, in the sacred Liturgy, we draw near not just to a manifestation of God's presence in the form of a cloud, but to the very body and blood of Our Lord Jesus Christ in the Blessed Sacrament. And we will receive our divine Lord sacramentally within us in holy communion.

We truly are not worthy to participate in all this. Indeed, our sinfulness stands in stark contrast to what we are about to do in the Mass. And so, the priest invites us to "prepare ourselves to celebrate the sacred mysteries" by humbly confessing our sins publicly before almighty God and the congregation. Just as the people of Israel needed to wash their garments before approaching the Lord at Sinai, so we need to cleanse our souls from sin before we approach God in the Mass. Indeed, washing is a biblical image for removal of sin: "Wash me thoroughly from my iniquity, and cleanse me from my sin...wash me, and I shall be whiter than snow" (Ps 51:2, 7).

## I Confess

The prayer known as the *Confiteor*—the first word of this prayer in Latin, meaning "I confess"—stands in a long biblical tradition of confessing one's sins. Sometimes, this was done in a formal public ceremony of repentance (Neh 9:2). Other times, it was the spontaneous response of an individual (Ps 32:5; 38:18). Confessing one's sins was encouraged in the wisdom books of the Bible (Prv 28:13; Sir 4:26), and the Old Testament law even required people to confess certain sins (Lv 5:5; Nm 5:7). Some individuals in the Old Testament, in an act of national repentance, confess the sins of all of Israel (Dn 9:20; Neh 1:6).

The practice of confessing one's sins continued in the New Testament, which begins with crowds following John the Baptist and confessing their sins in his baptism of repentance (Mt 3:6; Mk 1:5). The New Testament elsewhere exhorts Christ's followers to do the same. John teaches that we should confess our sins with confidence that the Lord will forgive us: "If we confess our sins, he is faithful and just, and will forgive our sins and cleanse us from all unrighteousness" (1 Jn 1:9). James exhorts us also to confess our sins to one another, asking each other for prayers that we may be freed from our sins: "Therefore confess your sins to one another, and pray for one another, that you may be healed" (Jas 5:16).

Since confessing sin was a common practice in ancient Israel and in the New Testament period, it is not at all surprising that the early Christians confessed their sins before partaking in the Eucharist. This is seen in one of the earliest non-biblical accounts we have about the Eucharist, found in an early second-century Christian text called the *Didache* (or "Teaching of the Apostles"): "Assemble on the Lord's Day, and break bread and offer the Eucharist; but first make confession of your faults, so that your sacrifice may be a pure one."[23] This early practice described in the *Didache* might itself reflect St. Paul's exhortation to "let a man examine himself" before partaking of the Eucharist, lest he do so in "an unworthy manner" (1 Cor 11:28, 27).

## An Examination of Conscience

In the *Confiteor*, we confess our sins not only "to almighty God," but also "to you my brothers and sisters." The prayer thus follows the exhortation of James to "confess your sins to one another" (Jas

---

[23] *Didache*, 14, as translated by Maxwell Staniforth in *Early Christian Writings* (New York: Penguin Books, 1987).

5:16), and it highlights the social effects of sin. Our sins affect our relationship with God *and* our relationships with each other.

The *Confiteor* also challenges us to consider seriously four areas in which we may have fallen into sin: "In my thoughts and in my words, in what I have done and what I have failed to do." These four points serve as an excellent examination of conscience:

First, *in my thoughts:* St. Paul exhorts us to guard our thoughts, keeping them focused on what is good: "Whatever is true, whatever is honorable, whatever is just, whatever is pure, whatever is lovely, whatever is gracious, if there is any excellence, if there is anything worthy of praise, think about these things." (Phil 4:8). Jesus, in the Sermon on the Mount, gives several warnings about ways we can fall into sin in our thoughts. For example, without ever physically harming someone, we can sin through our anger toward others (Mt 5:22). Without ever physically touching someone, we can fall into adultery of the heart through our lustful thoughts (Mt 5:27-28). Judging others (Mt 7:1), being anxious about the future, or falling into deep discouragement are other ways our thoughts can lead us into sin (see Mt 6:25-34).

Second, *in my words:* The letter of James warns us that the tongue is a fire. The spoken word can be used to bless and to curse, and when it is used for evil it causes great turmoil. "How great a forest is set ablaze by a small fire!" (Jas 3:5). The Bible mentions many ways our speech can be used for harm. For example, gossip (2 Cor 12:20; 1 Tm 5:13; Rom 1:29), slander (Rom 1:30; 1 Tm 3:11), insult (Mt 5:22), lying (Col 3:9; Wis 1:11; Sir 7:12-13) and boasting (Ps 5:5; 75:4; 1 Cor 5:6; Jas 4:16). These and other sins of speech are to be confessed in the *Confiteor.*

Third, *in what I have done:* This area encompasses what most people commonly think about sin—actions that directly hurt other people or our relationship with God. Along these lines, the Ten Commandments are often used as the basis for an examination of conscience.

Fourth, *in what I have failed to do:* This is the most challenging part. Not only are we responsible for the selfish, prideful, and evil actions we have committed, but we also will be held accountable on the Day of Judgment for the good that we failed to do! As the letter of James teaches, "Whoever knows what is right to do and fails to do it, for him it is sin" (Jas 4:17).

This part of the *Confiteor* reminds us that the Christian path is not merely a *via negativa* of avoiding sinful thoughts, words, desires, and actions. Christianity is ultimately about the *imitatio Christi*—the imitation of Christ. We must put on Christ and his virtues. Paul exhorts the Colossians to put on compassion, kindness, lowliness, meekness, patience—and most of all—love (Col 3:12-15). Jesus does not want us merely to avoid sin; he wants us to grow in his self-giving love.

This is why the sin of the Rich Young Man is so tragic. He was a very impressive Jewish man who kept all the commandments—no small feat, indeed! However, he was unwilling to answer the call of Christ. He could not let go of his possessions, give to the poor, and follow Jesus. And this was his downfall. Though he might have received an "A" on the first three levels of the *Confiteor*'s examination of conscience, he failed to pursue the higher good to which Jesus called him and therefore remained far from the kingdom of heaven (Mt 19:16-24). This part of the *Confiteor* at Mass challenges us to ask whether there is something in our lives—even if it is not bad—that, like the possessions of the Rich Young Man, has a hold on our heart and keeps us from following Christ's call.

## My Most Grievous Fault?

Finally, let us consider two points about the new translation of this prayer. Both improvements more adequately reflect the Latin text of the Mass and help underscore the seriousness of sin. First, instead of simply saying, "I have sinned" at the beginning of this prayer, we now say "I have *greatly* sinned." This reflects David's repentant words to God, "I have sinned greatly in that I have done this thing" (1 Chr 21:8). Second, instead of simply saying "through my own fault," we repeat it three times while striking our breasts in a sign of repentance:

> *"...through my fault, through my fault,*
> *through my most grievous fault."*

This repetition more fully expresses sorrow over our sins. When we are at fault over something small, we might simply say to the person whom we have wronged, "I'm sorry." But if it is a more serious matter and we *deeply* feel sorrow over our actions, we sometimes apologize several times and in varying ways: "I'm so sorry...I really regret doing that...Please forgive me." This line in the liturgy helps us recognize that sinning against God is no light matter. We must take responsibility for whatever wrong we have done, or the good that we should have done but failed to do. Therefore, at Mass, I do not simply offer an apology to God. In the *Confiteor*, I express heartfelt contrition and humbly admit that I have sinned "through my own fault, through my own fault, through my most grievous fault."

# 4. Lord, Have Mercy

*Priest:* Lord, have mercy.
*People:* Lord, have mercy.

*Priest:* Christ, have mercy.
*People:* Christ, have mercy.

*Priest:* Lord, have mercy.
*People:* Lord, have mercy.

This three-fold plea for God's mercy fittingly flows after the three-fold admission of one's sin in the previous prayer, the *Confiteor.* Coming near the beginning of the liturgy, it also parallels the three-fold affirmation of God's holiness sung later in the *Sanctus,* when we join the angels and saints in heaven who never cease to sing, "Holy, Holy, Holy Lord, God of hosts... ."

As we prepare ourselves to enter the sacred mysteries of the liturgy—to draw near the Thrice-Holy God—we do so in union with the Blessed Virgin Mary and all the angels and saints, as we pray in the *Confiteor.* In fear and awe over the divine presence drawing near and the joining of heaven and earth in the liturgy, we cannot help but ask for God's mercy. As one theologian explains, "All of us together come into his presence, together with angels and saints; and we ask him to show us his mercy and grant us his salvation. It bears repeating, insistence, even a kind of stammering: 'Lord, have mercy. Lord, have mercy. Christ, have mercy. Christ, have mercy. Lord, have mercy. Lord, have mercy.'"[24]

## The Meaning of Mercy

The Scriptures reveal several moving accounts about individuals crying out for God's mercy. Psalm 51, for example, stands out for its sincerity and vulnerability. In this psalm, David lays bare his heart before the Lord as he comes to terms with the truth of his sinful deeds. He admits his wrongdoing and begs,

> *"Have mercy on me, O God,*
> *according to thy steadfast love;*
> *according to thy abundant mercy*
> *blot out my transgressions.*
> *Wash me thoroughly from my iniquity,*
> *and cleanse me from my sin!*
> *For I know my transgressions,*
> *and my sin is ever before me...*
> *Against thee, thee only, have I sinned,*
> *and done that which is evil in thy sight..." (Ps 51:1-4a)*

But what does it mean to ask for God's mercy? This plea can often be misunderstood if we do not grasp clearly what mercy actually is. John Paul II once noted that mercy is sometimes mistakenly viewed as establishing "a relationship of inequality" between the one extending mercy and the one receiving it. God is thus seen as the Almighty King who merely pardons his wayward subjects.

---

[24] Driscoll, *What Happens at Mass*, p. 26.

### Not a Children's Game

In this faulty perspective, the plea "Lord have mercy" in the liturgy might be seen as similar to the cry for mercy in a game children play called by the same name: "Mercy." In this tournament of strength, two kids interlock hands and squeeze with all their might until the weaker one's wrist is twisted in pain and he begs his opponent to stop by crying out, "Mercy!"

Biblical mercy is not like that. Rather, the relationship of mercy is better exemplified by the parable of the Prodigal Son. In this story, the wayward son, suffering in his misery, begins to see the sinfulness of his actions. He humbly repents and returns home to his father. According to John Paul II, the father in the story "sees so clearly the good which has been achieved [in his son] thanks to a mysterious radiation of truth and love, that he seems to forget all the evil which the son had committed."[25] In this case, the father does not merely pardon his son for his offenses. Rather, he sees the good taking place in his son—his change of heart, his sorrow for his sins, and his noble desire to get his life back on track. And the father rejoices in seeing this good in his son and eagerly welcomes him back.

This reminds me of a time when I was watching two of my children playing in a different room, unaware of my presence. The older sister was four and the younger brother was two at the time. The little brother was playing with his favorite toy in his lap when, suddenly, the older one walked up to him and snatched the toy out of his hands, triumphantly ready to walk away with it.

My little boy predictably had a look of horror on his face and was about to wail. I was ready to march into the room to issue discipline for this injustice when I noticed the older sister do something incredible: She put the toy back in his hands and gave him a big hug, saying, "I'm so sorry! Here you are."

I couldn't believe my eyes! A second earlier, my blood pressure

---

[25]  John Paul II, *Dives et Misericordia*, no. 6.

was rising with the cries of my toddler who had his toy stolen from him. But now I saw that my daughter felt badly about what she had done and wanted to set things right. She clearly did not like the fact that she hurt her brother's feelings. She asked for his forgiveness. So instead of wanting to punish her, I now wanted to hug her! I saw not merely her wrongdoing (she took his toy). Even more, I saw her heart (she loves her brother, felt badly about hurting him, and sincerely apologized—all on her own initiative!).

I think this is similar to how our Heavenly Father views us when we sin and sincerely repent. He sees not just the legal fact of our sins. He also sees our contrite heart. As the Psalmist once said, "A broken and contrite heart, O God, thou wilt not despise" (Ps 51:17). Indeed, a sincerely sorrowful heart is irresistible to God. This is the proper context for understanding mercy. Mercy is not to be seen as a higher power like a monarch randomly pardoning criminals in his kingdom. It is about God's *love* for us, even in the face of our sins.

## Lord, Have Mercy

While the *Kyrie* is primarily an expression of repentance, it also can be seen as a petition, a prayer representing the cry of God's people for assistance in their lives.[26] Already in the fourth century, for example, the prayer "Lord, have mercy" (*Kyrie Eleison* in Greek) was the response of Greek Christians to petitions recited in the liturgy.[27]

This understanding reflects the New Testament use of the expression. In the gospels, many people approach Jesus asking for his mercy in the sense of pleading for healing and help in their lives. For example, two blind men come to Jesus, saying, "Have mercy on us, Son of David" (Mt 9:27; see also 20:30-31). The blind beggar Bartimaeus does the same (Mk 10:46-48; see Lk 18:38-39). Similarly,

---

[26] See Parsch, *The Liturgy of the Mass*, p. 95.

[27] See Joseph Jungmann, *The Mass* (Collegeville, MN: Liturgical Press, 1976), p. 168.

ten lepers call out to Christ, "Jesus, Master, have mercy on us," and Jesus cures them of their leprosy (Lk 17:13).

Along these lines, we can entrust to the Lord our own sufferings in the *Kyrie*, confident in the Lord's ability to assist us. This includes our physical ailments, our personal trials, and even our own *spiritual* blindness, weakness, and sin. Like the blind and lame who come to Jesus for help, we come to Mass with our own afflictions and trials, with our own inability to change—our spiritual and moral paralysis. We join the countless afflicted souls, from the time of Jesus to today, who have found comfort and strength when they cried out, "Lord, have mercy."

## Mercy for Others

The gospels also tell of people coming to Jesus requesting mercy not just for themselves, but also for those whom they love. A mother cries out to Jesus to help her daughter, saying, "Have mercy on me, O Lord, Son of David, my daughter is severely possessed by a demon" (Mt 15:22). A father desperately turns to Jesus on behalf of his son's troubles, saying "Lord, have mercy on my son, for he is an epileptic and he suffers terribly" (Mt 17:15).

We, too, can entrust to the Lord those we love every time we pray the *Kyrie* at Mass. Like the mother and father in the Bible, we can say "Have mercy on my friend who just lost his job"…"Have mercy on my neighbor who was just diagnosed with cancer"… "Have mercy on my son who left the Church"…"Have mercy on my daughter who is lonely, unhappy and lost in life." Thomas Howard offers this beautiful reflection on the power of the *Kyrie*:

> In the *Kyrie* …we may hear the fathomless cry of the whole race of man ascending to heaven from the depths. *Kyrie!* Goes up from all widows, and all dispossessed and brutalized children, and from all the maimed, and the prisoners and exiles, and from every sickbed, and indeed from all

wounded beasts, and we could believe, from all rivers and seas stained with man's filth and landscapes scarred by his plunder. In the liturgy, somehow, we stand before the Lord *on behalf of* his whole groaning creation.[28]

## Why Greek?

Many saints have reflected on the significance of the three-fold petition for God's mercy in the liturgy. Some have viewed this as an invocation of Jesus as our brother, our redeemer, and our God, while others have seen it as a reference to the Trinity, in the sense that we are asking each of the Divine Persons for mercy (Lord = Father; Christ = Son; Lord = Holy Spirit).

Traditionally, this prayer has been recited in Greek (*Kyrie eleison*). St. Thomas Aquinas noted that Greek was just one of three languages used in the liturgy; Hebrew (e.g., "Alleluia," "Amen") and Latin (the common liturgical language of the Western Church in his day) were used as well. For Aquinas, these three liturgical languages reflect the same three used on the sign on Christ's cross (see Jn 19:19-20). St. Albert the Great offered a different explanation for why the invocation for God's mercy is made in Greek rather than in the Latin used elsewhere in the liturgy:

> The faith came to us Latins from the Greeks; Peter and Paul came to the Latins from the Greeks and from them came salvation for us. And so that we may be mindful that this grace came to us from the Greeks, we preserve even now the very words and syllables with which the divine mercy was first invoked by the people. For we owe this reverence to the fathers, that the traditions which they instituted should be followed also by us.[29]

---

[28] Thomas Howard, *If Your Mind Wanders at Mass* (Steubenville, OH: Franciscan University Press, 1995).

[29] As quoted in Thomas Crean, *The Mass and the Saints* (San Francisco: Ignatius Press, 2008), pp. 44-5.

# 5. The *Gloria* and *Collect*

*"Glory to God in the highest,*
*and on earth peace to people of good will.*
*We praise you,*
*we bless you,*
*we adore you,*
*we glorify you,*
*we give you thanks for your great glory,*
*Lord God, heavenly King,*
*O God, almighty Father..."*

The tone of the liturgy now shifts from sorrowful repentance to joyful praise as we arrive at a prayer known as the *Gloria*. This prayer is typically sung, but it comes from no ordinary hymn book. The opening line of the *Gloria* is taken from the words sung by the angels over the fields of Bethlehem, announcing to the shepherds the good news of Christ's birth: *"Glory to God in the highest, and on earth peace among men with whom he is pleased"* (Lk 2:14).

It is fitting that we sing these words at the beginning of the Sunday liturgy (except in Advent and Lent), for there is a sense in which every Mass makes present the mystery of Christmas once again. As God was made manifest to the world in the baby Jesus some 2,000 years ago, so he is made present sacramentally upon our altars at the consecration in every Mass. We thus prepare ourselves to welcome Jesus by repeating the same words of praise that the angels used to herald Christ's coming in Bethlehem.

## A Biblical Mosaic

The rest of the *Gloria* continues to be saturated with words from Sacred Scripture. In fact, one could describe this prayer, which goes back to early Christianity, as a mosaic of biblical titles for God and common biblical expressions of praise. Any Christian in tune with the Scriptures will hear echoes from the Bible at every step of this prayer. Indeed, the Christian who prays the *Gloria* joins the great men and women throughout salvation history—and even the angels and saints in heaven—in their praise of God for his work of salvation and for his own glory.

The prayer follows a Trinitarian pattern, beginning with praise of the Father who is addressed as "God, almighty Father" and "heavenly King"—two common biblical titles for God. He is often called "God Almighty" (Gn 17:1; Ex 6:3) or "Lord Almighty" (Bar 3:1; 2 Cor 6:18) or just simply "the Almighty" (Ps 68:14; 91:1). In the book of Revelation, the angels and saints in heaven praise him over and over again as the "Lord God Almighty" (Rv 4:8; 11:17; 15:3; 19:6).

Similarly, the *Gloria* praises God as the heavenly King, which also points to God's omnipotence. Throughout Scripture, God is described as king (Ps 98:6; 99:4; Is 43:15), and as the King of Israel (Is 44:6), the King of glory (Ps 24:7-10), and even the great King over all gods (Ps 95:3). Addressing God as heavenly King in the *Gloria*, we recognize him as "King of kings" and express our acceptance of his reign in our lives.

## A Father First

By addressing the Lord as "almighty" and "heavenly King" in the *Gloria*, we praise him for his omnipotent reign over heaven and earth. Yet, as the *Catechism* explains, his omnipotence must be seen in the context of his Fatherhood—which is exactly what we do in the *Gloria*. We address him as "Lord God, heavenly King, O God, almighty *Father*." We do not stop with a mere mention of God's power and kingship. We go on to praise him ultimately as our heavenly Father. If God were merely an all-powerful king, we might get the impression that he could be like a dictator who arbitrarily wields his authority to do whatever he wants. But God has what the *Catechism* calls a "fatherly omnipotence."[30] Just as a good father wants what is best for his children, God's power is in perfect harmony with his loving will that always seeks what is good for us and that provides for all our needs.[31]

Recognizing how good our God is—seeing him as the loving Father who, though all-powerful, freely chooses to share his goodness with us—we cannot help but worship, and give thanks and praise. Like lovers who tell each other over and over in varying ways "I love you," we express our love for God, saying, "We praise you, we bless you, we adore you, we give you thanks for your great glory." Most interesting is the last line in which we praise God for his glory. This is an expression of pure praise—loving God not just for what he does for us, but for who he *is*, for his glorious goodness and love.

## A Story in Three Acts

The next part of the *Gloria*, in a sense, tells a story—the story of Christ. Like a three-act play, the *Gloria* sums up the story of Christ's saving work moving from 1) his coming, to 2) his redeeming death, to 3) his triumphant resurrection and ascension into heaven.

> *"Lord Jesus Christ, Only Begotten Son,*
> *Lord God, Lamb of God, Son of the Father,*

---

[30]  CCC 270.

[31]  "In God, power, essence, will, intellect, wisdom, and justice are all identical. Nothing therefore can be in God's power which could not be in his just will or his wise intellect" (CCC 271).

> *you take away the sins of the world,*
> *have mercy on us;*
> *you take away the sins of the world,*
> *receive our prayer;*
> *you are seated at the right hand of the Father,*
> *have mercy on us."*

In the "first act," Jesus is addressed as "Son of the Father" and the "Only Begotten Son," which recalls various New Testament texts that point to Jesus' divine Sonship (e.g., Jn 5:17-18; 10:30-38; 2 Cor 1:19; Col 1:13; Heb 1:1-2). Most particularly, these titles echo a dramatic line in the prologue of the fourth gospel that focuses our attention on the Incarnation—the mystery in which the Son of God became man. John begins his gospel with a beautiful, poetic reflection on the eternal Word who is God, who was with the Father in the beginning and through whom all things were made (Jn 1:1-4). At the climax of this reflection, John astonishingly announces that this divine, eternal Word "became flesh and dwelt among us" (Jn 1:14). The God of the universe actually took on a human nature! St. John, as an eyewitness to Christ's life, goes on to say of Jesus, the divine Word, that "we have beheld his glory, glory as of the *only Son from the Father*" (Jn 1:14; emphasis added).

Thus, when we address Jesus as the "only begotten Son" in the *Gloria*, we recognize him not merely as a teacher, messenger, or prophet sent from God. We use the rich theological language of St. John and join him in praising Jesus as the divine Son, the eternal Word, who was made flesh and dwelt among us.

## The Lamb and the King

In the "second act," the *Gloria's* reference to Jesus as "Lamb of God" moves the story forward to Christ's redemptive mission. It recalls the theme of the Lamb's triumph over sin and the devil in the book of Revelation (Rv 5:6-14; 12:11; 17:14) and the worship of the Lamb by the angels and saints in heaven (Rv 5:8, 12-13; 7:9-10;

14:1-3). By addressing Jesus with this title in the *Gloria*, we thus join the heavenly worship of the Lamb as revealed in the book of Revelation.

The *Gloria* also addresses Jesus, saying, "Lamb of God...you take away the sins of the world." In this line, we repeat the prophetic words of John the Baptist when he first saw Jesus passing by in John's gospel (Jn 1:29, see Chapter 23 on the *Agnus Dei*). These words reveal Jesus as the new Passover lamb, who offers up his life on the cross for our sins. Just as the lamb was sacrificed on that first Passover night in Egypt in order to spare Israel from death, so Jesus is the new Passover lamb who is sacrificed on Calvary in order to save all humanity from the curse of death caused by sin.

Finally, in the "third act," the *Gloria* reverently leads us to praise Jesus in the unique position of authority he now possesses in heaven: "You are seated at the right hand of the Father." This line recalls Mark's account of Jesus ascending into heaven where he "sat down at the right hand of God" (Mk 16:19). In the Bible, the right hand is the position of authority (see Ps 110:1; Heb 1:13). In the *Gloria*, we bear witness to Christ's reign over heaven and earth and his kingdom, which will have no end (Dn 7:14). And we humbly ask him to "receive our prayer" and "have mercy on us."

Notice how the whole mission of Jesus is summed up in this section of the *Gloria*. We move from the Son's Incarnation, to his paschal mystery, to his enthronement in heaven. We move from praising Jesus as the "Only Begotten Son" of the Father who became flesh and dwelt among us; to worshiping him as the "Lamb of God" who by his sacrifice takes away the sin of the world; to praising him in his triumph over sin and death as he is "seated at the right hand of the Father." Indeed, the very climax of salvation history can be summed up in the *Gloria*.

## From *Kyrie* to *Gloria*!

One liturgical theologian from the mid-twentieth century, Pius Parsch, called the *Gloria* "the joyful response to the pleading of the *Kyrie*." In the *Kyrie*, we express our need for salvation and God's mercy. In the *Gloria*, we joyfully express our gratitude for having received salvation from Christ. In this sense, the *Kyrie* allows us to enter the mystery of Advent as we express our longing for a savior, while the *Gloria* expresses the joy of Christmas, as we thank God for sending us his Son to redeem us.

> We come to Mass conscious of two things: that we stand greatly in need of redemption, and that we have actually been saved. When I think of the first, I recognize my own insignificance; when I realize the second truth, I perceive my strength; in the first I see my weakness and utter poverty, in the other I see my power and greatness. Let us put in the prayerful *Kyrie* our yearning for salvation. In the joyful Gloria let us sing out confidently of our redemption, celebrating thus in every Mass both Advent and Christmas.[32]

St. Albert the Great made a similar point about the *Gloria* as a response to the *Kyrie*: "It is as if [God] were saying, 'I will certainly answer your cries and I will send to you in the Sacrament the one whom I sent into the world to your fathers, that you may partake of him, and be drawn out from your evils and be filled with every good.'"[33]

---

[32] Parsch, *The Liturgy of the Mass*, pp. 105-6.
[33] St. Albert the Great in *The Mass and the Saints*, p. 47.

## A Counter-Cultural Prayer

In response to the narrative of Christ's saving mission, the *Gloria* now praises Jesus with three biblical titles: *the Holy One, the Lord,* and *the Most High.*

> *"For you alone are the Holy One,*
> *you alone are the Lord,*
> *you alone are the Most High,*
> *Jesus Christ,*
> *with the Holy Spirit,*
> *in the glory of God the Father. Amen."*

Calling Jesus "the Most High" recalls a biblical title for God as the supreme being over all other "gods" (Gn 14:18; Ps 7:17).

Similarly, the Old Testament commonly calls God "the Holy One of Israel," expressing, on one hand, God's nature as holy—completely other—and on the other hand, Israel's unique, intimate relationship with this completely separate, all-holy God (Ps 71:22; Prv 9:10; Is 1:4; Hos 11:9-11). The New Testament reveals Jesus as the Holy One. Jesus refers to Himself with this divine title in Revelation 3:7, and an angel gives him this title in Revelation 16:5. When many disciples leave Jesus over his teaching on the Eucharist, Peter remains faithful to Christ and acknowledges him as "the Holy One" (Jn 6:69). Even the demons recognize Jesus as "the Holy One" (Mk 1:24, Lk 4:34).

Perhaps most remarkable is the line "you alone are the Lord." Lord (*kyrios*) in the Bible is a title for God. But in the ancient Roman world, "Lord" was the title given to the emperor. Thus, while calling Jesus "Lord" associated him with God (1 Cor 8:6; Phil 2:11), it was also extremely counter-imperial. The New Testament proclaims that *Jesus* is Lord, not Caesar! Someone in the ancient Roman world who said that Jesus alone is the Lord would be seen as an enemy to the Roman Empire. Many early Christians, in fact, died for this belief, refusing to worship the emperor or the Roman gods. This line from the *Gloria* today challenges us to be loyal to Jesus Christ and his commandments above anything else in this world, whether it be a job, possessions, financial security, prestige, or family. "You alone are the Lord."

The *Gloria* concludes with mention of the Third Person of the Trinity: *the Holy Spirit.* Jesus Christ is praised "with the Holy Spirit, in the glory of God the Father." Thus, the hymn succinctly culminates with homage paid to the Holy Trinity.

After the *Gloria*, the priest invites the people to pray a prayer known as the *Collect*. This prayer gathers together the intentions of the people participating in the Mass and concludes the Introductory Rites.

Part III

# THE LITURGY OF THE WORD

The Church has often used the image of "two tables" to express the continuity between the two main parts of the Mass: the Liturgy of the Word and the Liturgy of the Eucharist. God's people are nourished first from the table of holy Scripture, which is proclaimed in the Liturgy of the Word. Then they are fed with the body of Our Lord at the table of the Eucharist.

While the Eucharist is the very body and blood of Jesus and the "source and summit" of the Christian life, the Scriptures lead us to a deeper communion with Jesus in the Eucharist. Pope Benedict XVI noted how these two parts of the Mass are not merely juxtaposed, but have an inner unity, so much so that, together, they form "one single act of worship":

> From listening to the word of God, faith is born or strengthened (cf. Rom 10:17); in the Eucharist the Word made flesh gives himself to us as our spiritual food. Thus, "from the two tables of the word of God and the Body of Christ, the Church receives and gives to the faithful the bread of life." ...Consequently it must constantly be kept in mind that the word of God, read and proclaimed by the Church in the liturgy, leads to the Eucharist as to its own connatural end.[34]

Sitting attentively at only one of these tables simply will not do. We need both the inspired word of God in Scripture and the Incarnate Word of God present in the Blessed Sacrament. In the 1500s, Thomas à Kempis, in his spiritual classic, *The Imitation of Christ*, expressed how much the soul longs to be nourished from *both* of these tables:

> Without these two I could not live, for God's Word
> is the light of my soul, and Your sacrament the Bread

---

[34]  Benedict XVI, *Sacramentum Caritatis* (Post-Synod Exhortation on the Eucharist as the Source and Summit of the Church's Life and Mission), p. 44.

of life. These can also be called the two tables placed
in the treasury of holy Church. One table is that of
the sacred altar on which rests the holy Bread that is
Christ's precious Body; the other is that of divine law
which contains holy doctrine, teaches the true faith,
lifts the veil of the sanctuary and leads us securely to
the holy of holies.[35]

## God's Word Spoke to You

Let us focus our attention now on the first table, the Liturgy of
the Word. The readings from Scripture do not merely provide us
with exhortations for moral living and reflections about the spiritual life. The Bible does not simply talk about God, but is God's
own speech. In the Liturgy of the Word, therefore, we encounter the
words of God Himself spoken personally to each one of us.

This does not mean the Scriptures are not human. They were
written by human beings, to particular human communities, at a
certain moment in history. Each book of the Bible contains the
human author's writing style, personality, theological outlook, and
pastoral concerns. But the Scriptures also are inspired by God.
"Inspiration" comes from the Greek word *theopneustos*, which
means "God-breathed" (2 Tm 3:16). In the inspired books of the
Bible, God breathed forth his divine words through the human
words of the sacred writers. Thus, Scripture is like Jesus Christ
Himself—fully human and fully divine. As Vatican II explained,
"To compose the sacred books, God chose certain men who, all
the while he employed them in this task, made full use of their own
faculties and powers so that, though he acted in them and by them,
it was as true authors that they consigned to writing whatever he
wanted written, and no more."[36]

To hear the words of God is a serious matter. At Mount Sinai,

---

[35] Thomas à Kempis, *Imitation of Christ*, 4, 11.
[36] *Dei Verbum* 11; CCC 106.

the people of Israel prepared themselves for three days before God spoke to them the words of the covenant. In the Mass, we prepare ourselves for this holy encounter with God's Word through the Introductory Rites—the sign of the cross, the *Confiteor*, the *Kyrie*, and the *Gloria*. Having marked ourselves with the sign of the cross, confessed our unworthiness to be in God's presence, asked for his mercy and sung his praises, we now sit down to listen carefully to what God wants to speak to us through his own inspired words in the Scriptures. And this is a personal encounter, for as Vatican II taught, "In the sacred books the Father who is in heaven comes lovingly to meet his children, and talks with them."[37]

In order to appreciate the profound nature of what is really happening in the Liturgy of the Word, consider the amazing role played by the lector who reads the Scriptures to us. The lector is not simply a public reader of the Bible. At Mass, the Lord uses the lector as the instrument through whom he proclaims his Word to the people. Think of this as the lector lending God his human voice so that God's words can be spoken to us at Mass. What an amazing honor and privilege it is to read the Word of God! And what a blessing it is for us to hear it (see Rv 1:3).[38]

## The Greatest Bible Study on Earth

The idea of having a cycle of readings from Scripture for liturgical worship is rooted in ancient Jewish practice. In the first century, the Law and the Prophets were regularly read in the context of synagogue worship.[39] And the rabbis of the early third century testify to a regular pattern of readings from the Law and the Prophets for worship in the synagogue, which may reflect what was

---

[37] *Dei Verbum*, no. 21.
[38] See Driscoll, *What Happens at Mass*, p. 40.
[39] See Lk 4:16-17; Acts 13:14-15; 15:21; Josephus, *AgAp* 2.17.175; Philo, *Somn* II 18. 127.

practiced in Jesus' day. Some of the rabbinic evidence even points to the possible use of a three-year cycle of readings.[40]

Similarly, the selections from Scripture read at our Sunday liturgy today are determined by a three-year cycle of readings from the various parts of the Bible: the Old Testament, the Psalms, the New Testament, and then the Gospel. Even the order of these readings has significance, for it reflects the order of God's redemptive plan. The readings ordinarily move from the Old to the New—from Israel to the Church. The proclamation of the Gospel comes at the climax, reflecting how Jesus is at the center of salvation history with all of Scripture pointing to him.

In a sense, the Mass is the greatest Bible study on earth. Simply by going to Mass on Sunday, Catholics are taken on a grand tour of the Sacred Scriptures that often highlights the connections between the Old and New Testaments. Weekday Masses follow a two-year cycle of readings that provide an even broader range of the Scriptures in the liturgy. These readings are not selected from among a pastor's or congregation's favorite parts of the Bible. Rather, priest and people are challenged with more of the totality of Word of God, covering all major parts of the Bible in a way that is not dependent on people's preferences or expertise.

## The Liturgical Year

The readings from Scripture also correspond to the various seasons and feasts of the Church. On one level, the Church walks us through the life and mission of Jesus through the seasons of the liturgical year. In the four weeks of Advent, we recall the Old Testament period of humanity's longing for the Savior. In the Christmas season, we rejoice in the birth of the Son of God who came to dwell among us. In the forty days of Lent, we participate in Jesus' prayer and fasting in the desert as we prepare to enter Christ's

---

[40]  *B. Meg.* 29b. See also James Aageson, "Lectionary" in *Anchor Bible Dictionary*, ed. David Noel Freedman et al. (New York: Doubleday, 1992), p. 271.

passion in Holy Week. In the fifty days of the Easter season, we celebrate Jesus' resurrection triumph and ascension into heaven, culminating on the fiftieth day with his sending of the Spirit on Pentecost. The rest of the liturgical year—known as Ordinary Time—focuses our attention on the public ministry of Jesus.

All throughout the year, the Church also draws our attention to the various mysteries of faith. The feast of *Corpus Christi* (literally, "body of Christ"), for example, celebrates the gift of the Eucharist. The feast of the Holy Trinity focuses on the mystery of the Godhead as Three Divine Persons. The Feast of All Saints praises God for the supernatural work he has accomplished in transforming weak, sinful human beings into saints, and reminds us of our own call to sanctity. Scattered throughout the year also are the feasts and memorials of the many saints who serve as models for us to follow in our own imitation of Christ. The Blessed Virgin Mary is chief among them and the saint most often commemorated in the Liturgical Year, as we celebrate her Immaculate Conception, her Nativity, her Assumption, and other aspects of her life and role in God's saving plan.

Certainly, we should praise the Lord for every aspect of his life, especially his death and resurrection, every day of the year. And we should be constantly thankful for the mysteries of faith and the saints he has given us. But we are human and cannot fully grasp the *entire* mystery of Christ at once. This is one reason why the Church marks off special days to give attention, thanks and praise for a particular aspect of Jesus' life or a specific aspect of the Catholic faith. As one liturgical scholar put it, "Each year [the Church] sees him an infant in the manger, fasting in the desert, offering Himself on the cross, rising from the grave, founding his Church, instituting the sacraments, ascending to the right hand of the Father, and sending the Holy Ghost upon men. The graces of all these divine mysteries are renewed in her."[41]

Journeying through the Church's Year annually throughout

---

[41]  Abbot Guéranger, *The Liturgical Year*, vol. 1, Book 1, p. 11.

one's life also helps us to appreciate Christ and his work of salvation all the more. It is similar to what happens when families celebrate birthdays, anniversaries, and other important dates and events. In my family, for example, we thank God each day for the blessing of each other's lives in a general way. But we also celebrate birthdays, which help the family rally together to honor a particular child and give special thanks for the gift of that person's life. Similarly, although I pray for my wife and my marriage every day of the year, celebrating our anniversary is an annual opportunity to thank God in a more particular way for the blessing of each other's lives and the sacramental bond we share.

As the Family of God, the Church fittingly marks off special days to celebrate birthdays, anniversaries, and other key aspects of God's plan of salvation. But in this supernatural family, it is Christ Himself who is present in the various yearly celebrations. As Pius XII taught,

> Hence, the liturgical year, devotedly fostered and accompanied by the Church, is not a cold and lifeless representation of the events of the past, or a simple and bare record of a former age. It is rather Christ Himself who is ever living in his Church. Here He continues that journey of immense mercy which He lovingly began in his mortal life, going about doing good, with the design of bringing men to know His mysteries and in a way live by them. These mysteries are ever present and active.[42]

---

[42]  Pius XII, *Mediator Dei*, no. 165.

# 6. The First Reading

The first reading is usually from the Old Testament (except during Easter Season, when it is from Acts of the Apostles, following an ancient practice). Although the Old Testament awaits the fullness of divine revelation in Jesus Christ, it is accepted by the Church with veneration as "authentic divine teaching." In the Old Testament, "the mystery of our salvation is present in a hidden way."[43] In fact, one cannot adequately understand Jesus and the New Testament Scriptures without knowing the story of Israel in the Old. For the New Testament is like the last chapter of a great book or the climactic scene in a great movie. The more one grasps the many dramatic twists and turns in the story that went before—the Old Testament story of Israel—the more one will be able to understand of the climax of the story of Jesus Christ and his Kingdom in the New.

The inclusion of the Old Testament reading at Mass helps us to enter into that story of Israel and thus see the unity of the Bible more clearly.[44] For as Vatican II taught, echoing St. Augustine, God "brought it about that the New should be hidden in the Old and that the Old should be manifest in the New. For, although Christ founded the New Covenant in his blood...still the books of the Old Testament, all of them caught up into the Gospel message, attain

---

[43]  *Dei Verbum*, no. 16.

[44]  Apostolic Constitution *Missale Romanum* (April 3, 1969).

and show forth their full meaning in the New Testament...and, in their turn, shed light on it and explain it."[45]

These readings generally correspond to the Gospel reading for the day. Sometimes, the correspondence is thematic, illustrating continuity or contrast between the Old Testament story and the Gospel. Other times, the readings underscore how the Old Testament prefigures Christ and the Church. Images of Passover are associated with readings about the Eucharist. The Exodus story is linked with baptism. As such, the beautiful symphony of Scripture resounds in the Liturgy of the Word.

## Thanks Be To God

At the end of the first reading, the lector says "The Word of the Lord." One theologian has noted that this announcement is like a great shout or a trumpet call, reminding us how marvelous it is for us human beings to hear God speak to us through the Scriptures: "The declaration should be heard with absolute amazement. How absurd it would be to take for granted that God should speak in our midst. We are expressing our amazement, and we are saying that we do not take it for granted when we cry out from the depths of our hearts, 'Thanks be to God.'"[46]

Thanksgiving is gratitude to God for his goodness and his acts in history. It is a common facet of worship in the Bible from the Old Testament (1 Chr 16:4; Ps 42:4, 95:2) to the New (Col 2:7; 4:2). The specific words, "Thanks be to God," were used by St. Paul to thank the Lord for delivering him from sin and death (Rom 7:25; 1 Cor 15:57; 2 Cor 2:14). Since the whole of the Bible ultimately points to Christ's work of salvation, it is fitting that we respond to the Scriptures proclaimed in the liturgy with the same expression

---

[45]  *Dei Verbum*, no. 16.
[46]  Jeremy Driscoll, *What Happens at Mass*, pp. 40-41.

of gratitude St. Paul used in his joyful thanksgiving for Christ's victory on the cross: "Thanks be to God!"

Our response is then followed by a moment of silence as we sit in awe and adoration of the God who just spoke to us. Silence is part of the heavenly liturgy in the book of Revelation (Rv 8:1), and it gives us time to reflect on the words we just heard—to become like Mary who "kept all these things, pondering them in her heart" (Lk 2:18).

# 7. The Responsorial Psalm

After hearing God's word proclaimed in the first reading, we respond next, not with our own meager, human words, but with God's own inspired words of praise and thanksgiving from the book of Psalms. The recitation—or, even better, the singing—of the psalms helps to create an atmosphere of prayer conducive for meditation on the reading. Using the psalms in our worship of God is quite natural. St. Paul exhorted his followers to sing psalms (Col 3:16). And the tradition of using psalms for liturgical worship goes back even further.

The book of Psalms represents a collection of 150 sacred hymns used for private devotion and public worship in the Temple liturgy. In the Temple, the verses of the psalms would be sung by two alternating groups with a common refrain (the antiphon) that was sung before and after the psalm itself. We see some indications of this in the book of Psalms itself. Some psalms, for example, include the aside "Let Israel now say..." (Ps 124:1; 129:1), which seems to be a rubric inviting the assembly to respond. We see this also in Psalm 136. This psalm starts with the call to "Give thanks to the Lord, for he is good," and the subsequent verses list various reasons for being thankful to God. Each of those verses begins with an opening line such as "to him who alone does great wonders" or "to him who led the people through the wilderness." And each ends with the same repeated refrain: "For his steadfast love endures forever." This calling back and forth between motive and response points to a kind of liturgical dialogue, with the opening words being recited by a leader and the refrain serving as the response given by the people.

This back-and-forth or "antiphonal" movement is found not only in the Responsorial Psalm, but throughout the Mass: "The Lord be with you…And also with you." "The word of the Lord… Thanks be to God." "Lift up your hearts…We lift them up to the Lord." It is also found throughout the Bible. Moses, in the covenant ceremony at Sinai, proclaims the words of the Lord to the people, and they all answer liturgically, "in one voice," saying, "All that the Lord has spoken we will do" (Ex 19:8). When Ezra read the book of the law to the people, he blessed the Lord and the people responded "Amen, Amen" (Neh 8:6). When St. John, in the book of Revelation, has a vision of the liturgy in heaven, he sees thousands of angels praising the Lord by saying, "Worthy is the Lamb who was slain, to receive power and wealth and wisdom and might and honor and glory and blessing!" Then, all the creatures reply, "To him who sits upon the throne and to the Lamb be blessing and honor and glory and might for ever and ever!" And the angelic four living creatures answer back, "Amen" (Rv 5:11-14).

These heavenly shouts of praise and affirming replies express the awe-filled joy of the angels and saints in the presence of God. Thomas Howard comments that it is similar to the excitement we experience when we find someone who shares one of our deep convictions—when we hear that person say something with which we wholeheartedly agree, something we are passionate about, maybe even something that expresses a sentiment or belief that we could not have expressed better ourselves. When someone says something that strikes a deep chord within us, we cannot help but express our joyful agreement. We feel the need to join in the conversation and affirm the statement: "Yes! That's exactly right!"

Indeed, there is great joy in being in the company of others who agree on matters most important us. The angels and saints in heaven possess this kind of joyful agreement to an even greater degree. Standing in the presence of the goodness and love of God, they cannot help but praise and thank him. And they seem to have the need to affirm and echo each other's words of praise and thanksgiving. Some begin glorifying God, saying "Worthy is the Lamb... to receive...honor and glory and blessing!" Others in wholehearted agreement answer with resounding praise: "To the Lamb be blessing and honor and glory." And still others don't want to be left out. They, too, must declare that they share these sentiments as they cry out "Amen!" Howard envisions this back-and-forth praise of God by all the angels, saints, and creatures in the book of Revelation as "a dance" which we are invited to join during the Mass.

> The universe, all creatures and things, all angels and saints, invite us, "Come, join the Dance." The antiphons of the Mass are early training in *the* great choreography, in *the* great ringing antiphon before the eternal *perichoresis*, the "Dance" of the Persons of the Trinity. The seraphim know this; and in the liturgy we begin to be introduced into this blissful antiphonality. When we respond to the Psalm, we are taking our first steps in the Dance. [47]

Clearly, the liturgical dialogue in the Mass follows a biblical model for worship, even more, a heavenly model for worship. It is no wonder, therefore, that the early Christians picked up on this pattern and incorporated it into their worship of God. At least as early as the third century, psalms were being recited at Mass with cantors singing the psalms and the people giving a response, oftentimes repeating the first line of the psalm[48]—a practice that might reflect the way the psalms were used in ancient Israelite worship. All of this serves as the basis of our Responsorial Psalm today.

---

[47] Thomas Howard, *If Your Mind Wanders at Mass*, pp. 74-5.
[48] Hippolytus, *Trad. Ad..*, 515; Tertullian, *De or.*, c. 27. As cited in Charles Belmonte, *Understanding the Mass*, p. 87.

# 8. The Second Reading

The second reading comes from the New Testament: one of the epistles, the Acts of the Apostles, or the book of Revelation. Though often selected independently of the first reading and the Gospel, these New Testament writings reflect on the mystery of Jesus Christ and his saving work and the meaning it has for our lives. They also draw out the practical applications of our life in Christ and exhort us ever more to "put on Christ" and turn away from sin.

# 9. The Gospel

W hile the whole of the Bible is inspired, Vatican II taught that the gospels rightly have "a special place…because they are our principal source for the life and teaching of the Incarnate Word, our Savior."[49] The Mass reflects this preeminence. Notice how the liturgy shows special reverence to the reading of the Gospel. For this particular reading the priests, deacons, and people do things that they did not do for the other readings from Scripture.

*Standing:* First, the people stand to welcome the Lord Jesus who is about to be proclaimed in the Gospel reading. Standing was the reverent posture of the assembled Jews when Ezra read from the book of the law (Neh 8:5). As we prepare to hear Jesus speak to us in the Gospel, it is fitting that we welcome him in this way, expressing our reverence and our readiness to listen to him.

*Alleluia:* Second, the people say or sing "Alleluia," which is a Hebrew expression of joy meaning, "Praise Yahweh!" or "Praise the Lord!"[50] It is found at the beginning or end of many Psalms (Ps 104-106; 111-113; 115-117; 146-150), and was used by the angels in heaven to praise God for his work of salvation and to announce the coming of Christ to his people in the wedding supper of the Lamb

---

49   *Dei Verbum*, no. 18
50   The joyful "Alleluia" is not used in the penitential season of Lent. Another acclamation has been used such as, "Glory and praise to you, Lord Jesus Christ" or "Praise to you, Lord Jesus Christ, King of endless glory."

(Rv 19:1-9). This joyful praise is a fitting way to welcome Jesus who will come to us in the Gospel.

*Procession:* Third, during the Alleluia, the deacon or priest begins to process in the sanctuary, taking the Book of the Gospels from the altar to the lectern from where the reading will be proclaimed. Altar servers carrying candles and incense accompany the Book of the Gospels in this procession, further underscoring the solemnity of what is about to happen. To prepare himself for the sacred task of reading the Gospel, the priest quietly prays at the altar: "Cleanse my heart and my lips, almighty God, that I may worthily proclaim your holy Gospel." (If a deacon reads the Gospel, the priest recites a similar prayer for him at the beginning of the procession.) This prayer recalls how the prophet Isaiah's lips needed to be purified before he proclaimed the word of the Lord to Israel. When an angel touched his mouth with a burning coal, Isaiah's sin was forgiven and he was then called to begin his prophetic ministry (see Is 6:1-9).

*Sign of the Cross:* After another greeting dialogue ("The Lord be with you...And with your spirit") the priest or deacon announces the Gospel reading ("A reading from the holy Gospel according to John") and traces the sign of the cross on his forehead, mouth, breast, and on the book. The people also make the three-fold sign of the cross over themselves, a ritual by which we consecrate our thoughts, words, and actions to the Lord, asking that his Word in the Gospel be always on our minds, on our lips, and in our heart.

### Encountering Jesus

All this ceremony—standing, alleluia, procession, candles, incense, and the three-fold sign of the cross—shouts out to us that we are approaching a most sacred moment in the Mass. And that moment finally arrives when the Gospel is read. These Gospel accounts are not simply stories from the past, a distant record of memories about Jesus. Since Scripture is inspired by God, the gospels consist of God's own words about Christ's life. As the Church has taught, "when the Sacred Scriptures are read in the Church, God himself speaks to his people, and Christ, present in his own word, proclaims the Gospel."[51]

The proclamation of the Gospel, therefore, makes Jesus' life present to us in a profound way. We are not spectators in the pew hearing *about* what Jesus once said and did a long time ago in Palestine. We are not listening to a news report about Jesus or to a lecture about a famous religious figure from the first century. Christ speaks personally to each one of us through the divinely inspired words in the Gospel. For example, we do not merely hear *about* Jesus calling people to repent and follow him; we hear Jesus Himself say *to us* "Repent for the kingdom of heaven is at hand" (Mt 4:17). We do not simply hear *about* Jesus forgiving a woman who was caught in adultery. It is as if we hear Jesus say *to us* in our sorrow over our sins, "Neither do I condemn you; go, and do not sin again" (Jn 8:11).

---

[51] *General Instruction of the Roman Missal*, no. 29 (Washington, DC: USCCB Publishing, 2002).

# 10. The Homily

From the earliest days of Christian liturgy, the Word of God was not read on its own. It was accompanied by a homily which explained the meaning of the Scriptural readings and drew out the application for people's lives. The word *homily* means "explanation" in Greek. In the early Church, the bishop typically was the one who celebrated Sunday Mass and gave the homily. From this primitive practice came the homilies of St. Augustine, St. Ambrose, St. John Chrysostom, and many other celebrated texts from the Church Fathers.

Yet the liturgical practice of explaining Scripture readings did not start with Christianity. It is rooted in ancient Jewish custom. In the book of Ezra, for example, the book of the law was not merely read to the people. The Levites "helped the people to understand the law" (Neh 8:7). They read from God's law "and they gave the sense, so that the people understood the reading" (Neh 8:8).

The Jewish synagogues followed a similar practice. Readings from Scripture were accompanied by explanations. Jesus Himself practiced this custom. He expounded on a reading from Scripture in his hometown synagogue in Nazareth (see Lk 4:18-30), and he also regularly taught in the synagogues throughout Galilee (see Mk 1:21; Lk 4:15).

The homily is crucial for the instruction of the faithful, so that they can understand the readings and apply it to their lives. So important is the homily for passing on the faith that Vatican II taught that the homily should hold "pride of place" among the various forms of Christian instruction.[52]

## Who Gives the Homily?

Finally, the homily is to be given only by an ordained minister: a deacon, priest, or bishop. The same is true for the reading of the Gospel at Mass. While the other Scripture readings may be proclaimed by religious or laity, only a deacon, priest, or bishop is to read the Gospel. As a successor of the apostles, the bishop—and the priests and deacons with whom he shares his authority—have the responsibility to proclaim the Gospel and pass on all that Christ taught the apostles (Mt 28:18-20). Since the gospels are the heart of the Bible, reserving the Gospel reading for ordained ministers reminds us how *all* the readings from Scripture to which the gospels point "are to be read and understood under the authority of apostolic faith."[53]

This sheds light on why the homily, too, is to be delivered only by an ordained minister. A lay person or religious brother or sister certainly might have greater speaking abilities or more theological and spiritual points to offer on a given topic than a particular priest or deacon. And there are many ways for those gifts to be shared with the community. But that is not the purpose of the homily at Mass. While a homily ideally would be thoughtful, clear, and engaging, it ultimately is not a matter of eloquence or insight. Driscoll notes that the homily being given by an ordained minister is meant to be a sign or "guarantee" that the preaching is passing on "the Church's apostolic faith and not merely the private thoughts and experiences of an individual."[54] Although God's people as a whole are to give witness to the faith of the Church, it is the particular

---

[52] *Dei Verbum*, no. 24.

[53] Jeremy Driscoll, *What Happens at Mass*, p. 51.

[54] Ibid., p. 52.

responsibility of the bishop as a successor of the apostles to teach the apostolic faith. And his union with the pope and the other bishops throughout the world gives further visible, concrete witness to the apostolic faith. Since priests and deacons, by virtue of their ordination, share in this particular responsibility, they also may proclaim the Gospel and deliver the homily at Mass.

# 11. The Creed

The Creed is a summary statement of the faith used in the early Church as a rule or standard for Christian belief. Originally part of the rite of baptism for catechumens to profess the faith of the Church, the creeds later served as a means for ensuring right doctrine and curbing heresy.

But since the Creed is not itself from Scripture, one might wonder, "Why is this non-biblical text included in the Liturgy of the Word?" In response, we should note that the Creed summarizes the story of Scripture. Moving from creation to Christ's incarnation, death and resurrection, to the sending of the Holy Spirit, to the era of the Church and finally to the Second Coming, the Creed carries us through the entire story of salvation history. In one short statement of faith, we draw out the narrative thread from Genesis to the book of Revelation: creation, fall, redemption. And we do so with a keen eye to the three divine Persons who are the principle actors in this drama: the Father, the Son, and the Holy Spirit. As one theologian has commented, "What the Scriptures say at length, the creed says briefly."[55]

---

[55] Nicholas Lash, *Believing Three Ways in One God: A Reading of the Apostle's Creed* (London, England: SCM Press, 1992), 8, as cited in Gerard Loughlin, *Telling God's Story: Bible, Church and Narrative Theology* (New York: Cambridge University Press, 1996), p. 50.

## The Old Testament "Creed"

The practice of prayerfully reciting a creed has deep biblical roots. Ancient Israel was called to profess their faith in a creedal statement known as the *Shema*, the Hebrew word for "hear," which represents the first word of this prayer: "Hear, O Israel: The Lord our God is one Lord; and you shall love the Lord your God with all your heart, and with all your soul, and with all your might" (Dt 6:4-5). These sacred words were to be constantly on the people's hearts, taught to their children, and recited regularly throughout the day: in the morning when they wake, at night when they fall asleep, when in their homes, when they go out on the streets (Dt 6:6-10).

The *Shema* told a very different kind of story about the world than what was commonly known by the peoples surrounding Israel. Most ancient near eastern peoples held a polytheistic worldview: they believed there were many gods, and each tribe or nation had its own set of deities whom they needed to appease and keep happy. In this perspective, religion was typically tribal, ethnic, or national.

In this highly polytheistic environment surrounding Israel, the words "The Lord our God is *one* Lord" would be a bold, counter-cultural expression of Israel's monotheistic belief. But for the ancient Jews, this was not simply an abstract view about how many deities exist (only one). Jewish monotheism had a subversive edge. It proclaimed not only that there was one God, but that this one God was in a special covenant with Israel. In other words, *Israel's* God was not merely one god among the many deities in the world, but the one, true God over all the nations. Accordingly, Jewish monotheism unmasked the deities of the Egyptians, Canaanites, and Babylonians, for example, and showed them to be what they truly are: false gods, not deities at all! *Israel's* God was the only God.

We must see the Creed we recite at Mass as our *Shema*. Like the *Shema* of old, our creed has a counter-cultural message today. It tells a very different kind of story about life than what is commonly taught in the modern, secular world. Ours is an era of relativism—

the view that there is no moral or religious truth, no right or wrong. The relativistic worldview claims it does not matter what one believes about God or what one chooses to do with one's life. Since life has no real meaning, everybody should be free to make up their own moral and religious values and do whatever they want with their lives.

## The Cosmic Battle

In this "anything goes" cultural milieu, the Creed grounds us in reality and reminds us that our beliefs and choices do matter. Progressing from Creation to the redemptive work of Christ to the sanctifying mission of the Church today, the Creed presumes a narrative framework to human history. In other words, the Creed assumes that there is a plot to life, and that we are here for a reason. It proclaims that the universe is not here by random chance, but was brought into existence by the one true God, "the maker of heaven and earth," and is moving in a certain direction according to God's plan. The Creed also presumes that this divine plan was fully revealed in God's Son, the "one Lord Jesus Christ" who "became man" to show us the pathway to happiness and eternal life.

The Creed also notes how Jesus came "For us men and for our salvation" and to bring "forgiveness of sins." This admission that we needed to be saved and forgiven tells us that something went terribly wrong with our situation before the coming of Christ. It points to the original rebellion against God by Satan and his minions and to how they led Adam and Eve in the garden and the rest of the human family to participate in his rebellion by falling into sin. Thus, the story of the Creed implicitly tells of an intense conflict that has been raging since the beginning of time. It is a battle between good and evil, between God and the serpent (Gn 3:15; Rv 12:1-9), between what St. Augustine called "the City of God" and "the City of Man" and what John Paul II called the "civilization of love" and the "culture of death."

Thus, the Creed reminds us that our little lives are caught up into this much larger story. And we each have a significant role to play in this drama. The question is: "How well will I play my part?" The Creed will not let us persist in the modern relativistic myth that says there are no right or wrong choices, that it doesn't matter what we believe or what we do with our lives. The Creed reminds us that at the end of our lives we will stand before the Lord Jesus Christ who "will come again in glory to judge the living and the dead." And at that moment, all our life choices will be weighed in a balance before the divine judge, and we will receive our just reward or punishment for how we lived.

So the Creed will not let us be lukewarm bystanders in this cosmic struggle. It challenges us to pick what side of the conflict we will fight for. Will we follow the prince of this world who wants us to think there is no right or wrong? Or will we follow the King of heaven and earth who leads us to happiness in his everlasting kingdom? When we profess our faith at Mass in the Creed, we publicly stand before the whole congregation and Almighty God and plant the flag with Jesus. We solemnly declare that we will strive not to live like the rest of the world, but to give our wholehearted allegiance to the Lord: "I believe in one God..."

### The Two Sides of Belief

But why do we need to repeat this same profession of faith week after week? Why do we need to come back every Sunday and say "Yes, I still believe all this"? The key word at the start of the Creed that unites the various statements of faith will shed light on the weekly recitation of the Creed in the Mass. That key word is "believe."

According to the *Catechism*, there are two aspects of belief. On one hand, belief is something intellectual. It is *"a free assent to the whole truth that God has revealed."*[56] This aspect is what is most ob-

---

[56] CCC 150 (emphasis in original).

vious in the Creed. We affirm our belief that there is "one God," that Jesus is "the Only Begotten Son of God" and that he died and rose again on the third day. We also believe in "the Holy Spirit" and "one, holy, catholic, and apostolic Church" to which our minds give assent in all that she officially teaches.

On the other hand, even more fundamental to faith is its being "a personal adherence...to God."[57] One Hebrew word for belief ('aman), from which we derive the word "Amen," expresses this point. The word can be understood as meaning to take one's stand on something else.[58] In other words, from the Old Testament perspective, belief in God does not simply express an intellectual conviction that God exists. It also means a personal entrusting of one's life to God. It expresses how God is truly the foundation for my life.

### Marriage and a Math Equation

The difference between these two aspects of faith—the personal and the intellectual—is like the difference between a math equation and a marriage. If someone says, "I believe 2 + 2 = 4," he is saying that he thinks this statement is true. However, when a husband says to his wife, "Honey, I believe in you," he is not merely affirming his belief that she exists. He is saying "I believe in you...I entrust myself to you...I give my life to you."

Similarly, when we say in the Creed that "We believe in one God..." we are expressing something quite personal. More than simply affirming that God exists—though we certainly do that, too—we are also saying that we entrust our entire lives to the One who makes all the difference for us. This is one reason why we recite the Creed every Sunday at Mass. Just as married couples may affirm their trust and commitment to each other and regularly tell

---

[57] Ibid.

[58] See Joseph Ratzinger, *Introduction to Christianity* (San Francisco: Ignatius Press, 1990), p. 39.

each other "I love you," so do we in the Creed renew our commitment to the Lord each week, lovingly telling him over and over
again that we give ourselves to him, that we entrust our entire lives
to him—that we "believe" in him.

With this biblical sense of belief in mind, we can clearly see
that the Creed is not merely a list of doctrines on a sheet a paper
that need to be checked off. The "I believe…" in the Creed invites
us to surrender more and more of our lives to God each week. It
challenges us to ask, "Who is really at the center of my life? In whom
do I really place my trust?" When confronted with the words of the
Creed, we can ask ourselves, "Do I truly seek *God's* will for my life?
Or am I seeking *my* will first, running more after my own desires,
dreams, and plans?" "Do I truly surrender my life to the Lord? Or
are there areas of my life that are not consistent with the way of
Jesus?" "Do I trust my cares to his providential care? Or am I afraid
to give up control of my life and rely more on God?" Though none
of us have perfect faith, when we recite the Creed, we express our
desire to grow in our faith in God—to entrust *more* of our lives
to him. To put our total trust in anything or anyone else—our
abilities, our plans, our possessions, a career, a politician, a friend—
would be foolish and end in disappointment. Only God is worthy
of our total trust. The *Catechism* makes this point: "As personal
adherence to God and assent to his truth, Christian faith differs
from our faith in any human person. It is right and just to entrust
oneself wholly to God and to believe absolutely what he says. It
would be futile and false to place such faith in a creature."[59]

## "Consubstantial with the Father"

In closing, the Creed in the new English translation of the
Mass has a number of changes in vocabulary. I will mention just
a few. First, the new translation unites us more with the rest of the
Western world in using the singular "I" for its opening: "*I* believe

---
[59] CCC 150.

in one God." After Vatican II, English was the only major Western language that translated the singular "I believe" in the Latin (*Credo*) with the plural "*We* believe." The singular "I," however, makes the Creed more personal and challenges each individual to interiorize the faith. As the *Catechism* explains, "I believe" expresses "the faith of the Church professed personally by each believer."[60] This is what we do when we renew our baptismal promises at a baptism or at Easter. Each individual answers for himself. The bishop, priest, or deacon says, "Do you reject Satan?" And we each respond, "I do."

Second, instead of saying God is the maker "of all that is seen and unseen" as in the old translation, we now say he is the maker "of all things visible and invisible," which more accurately reflects the language of St. Paul who referred to the creation of all things "in heaven and on earth, visible and invisible" (Col 1:16).

Third, some technical, Christological language found in the Latin text for the Mass is now retained in the new translation. The previous translation referred to Jesus as "one in being with the Father," but we now speak of Jesus being "consubstantial with the Father." This more closely reflects the theological language of the Council of Nicea (A.D. 325) which clarified that the Son was "of the same substance" (in Greek, *homoousios*) as the Father and condemned the teaching of a man named Arius. He taught that Jesus "came to be from things that were not" and that he was "from another substance" than that of the Father.[61] Though the transliteration "consubstantial" might not roll off the tongue easily for some modern men and women, the use of this term in the Creed is more precise and provides an opportunity to reflect more on the divine nature of Christ and the Trinity.

Another important theological term is now preserved in the Creed's statement about Jesus' unique conception. The older translation referred to the Son in this way: "By the power of the Holy Spirit he was born of the virgin Mary, and became man." The

---

[60] CCC 167.
[61] See CCC 465.

new translation more accurately reflects the Latin text of the Mass which includes the theological Latin word *incarnatus* (Incarnate), which refers to "the fact that the Son of God assumed a human nature in order to accomplish our salvation in it."[62] In the words of John's gospel, "The Word became flesh" (Jn 1:14). Accordingly, we now say that the Son, "by the Holy Spirit was incarnate of the Virgin Mary, and became man." Not only is this a more precise translation; it also captures more of the theological point expressed in the Creed. The Son of God was not just born of the Virgin Mary. The Eternal Son of God who is of the same substance as the Father actually took on human flesh!

---

[62]  CCC 461.

# 12. The Prayer of the Faithful

The Liturgy of the Word culminates in what is known as "The Prayer of the Faithful." This is one of the most ancient parts of the Mass, already attested to by St. Justin Martyr in A.D. 155. St. Justin wrote to the Roman emperor explaining what Christians did at Mass, giving an outline of the prayers and rituals. In this letter, he described the intercessory prayers offered after the readings from Scripture and the homily: "Then we all rise together and offer prayers for ourselves…and for all others, wherever they may be, so that we may be found righteous by our life and actions, and faithful to the commandments, so as to obtain eternal salvation."[63]

This, of course, is quite similar to the "Prayer of the Faithful" we have in the Mass today—intercessory prayers that stand in a tradition that goes back at least to Justin Martyr's time in the second century.

But the practice of intercessory prayer goes back even further in Christian history. When Peter was imprisoned by Herod, the church in Jerusalem offered up "earnest prayer for him," and that night an angel came to release him from his chains (Acts 12:1-7). When St. Paul gave instructions to his disciple Timothy, he told him to intercede for all people: "I urge that supplications, prayers, intercessions, and thanksgivings be made for all men, for kings and all who are in high positions, that we may lead a quiet and peaceable life, godly and respectful in every way. This is good, and it is

---

[63] Justin Martyr, *Apol.* I, 67 as quoted in CCC 1345.

acceptable in the sight of God our Savior, who desires all men to
be saved and to come to the knowledge of the truth" (1 Tm 2:1-4).
Paul himself prayed constantly for the needs of his communities
(1 Thess 1:2-3) and pleaded with them to pray for his ministry (2
Cor 1:11). With this strong call for intercessory prayer in the New
Testament, it is fitting that general intercessions formally found a
home in the Mass from the earliest centuries of Christianity.

## Priestly Intercession

These general intercessions at Mass represent a significant
moment for the faithful. The *General Instruction of the Roman
Missal* notes that in these intercessions, the faithful "exercise their
priestly function."[64] That all of God's people—ordained priests,
religious, and laity—are given a priestly role is well attested in
Scripture. We are "a chosen race, a royal priesthood" (1 Pt 2:9), for
Christ has made us "a kingdom [of] priests" (see Rv 1:5-6). One
way our priestly office is exercised in the Mass is in the prayers
of the faithful, whereby we participate in Christ's priestly prayer
for the entire human family. Jesus poured out his heart in loving
intercession for the whole world (Jn 17). He is able to save others
"who draw near to God through him, since he always lives to
make intercession for them" (Heb 7:25). We participate in Christ's
intercession in a particular way at this moment of the liturgy.

The *Catechism* notes that intercessory prayer is "characteristic
of a heart attuned to God's mercy."[65] If we are truly in tune with
God's heart, we will naturally want to pray for others. The culmination of the Liturgy of the Word is a fitting time to offer up these
intercessions. Up to this point in the Mass, the faithful have heard
the Word of the Lord proclaimed in Scripture, expounded upon in
the homily and summed up in the Creed. Now, having been formed
in God's Word, the faithful respond with the heart and mind of

---

[64]   *General Instruction of the Roman Missal*, no. 45.
[65]   CCC 2635.

Jesus by praying for the needs of the Church and the world. Since the prayers are meant to be universal in scope—for those in authority, for those experiencing various needs and sufferings, and for the salvation of all—the intercessions train us to look not only after our own interests, "but also to the interests of others" (Phil 2:4).

Part IV

# THE LITURGY OF THE EUCHARIST

In the second half of the Mass, called the Liturgy of the Eucharist, Jesus' sacrifice on the cross is made present by the priest, who carries out what Jesus did at the Last Supper and what he commanded the apostles to do in his memory. In the Liturgy of the Eucharist, bread and wine are offered as gifts by the people and then consecrated and changed into the body and blood of Christ, which we receive in holy communion. We will consider this section in its three principal parts: 1) the Preparation of the Gifts; 2) the Eucharistic Prayer; and 3) the Communion Rite.

# A. The Preparation of the Gifts

The presentation of the gifts in the liturgy has its roots in the early Church. Already in A.D. 155, St. Justin Martyr mentioned the custom of someone bringing bread and wine to the priest after the prayers of intercession.[66] St. Hippolytus (A.D. 225) notes the practice as well. As the ritual developed, the faithful or a representative would process toward the altar to present a wide range of gifts in addition to bread and wine, such as oil, honey, wool, fruit, wax, or flowers. The bread and wine were used in the Eucharistic liturgy, while other gifts were given to support the priests or to serve the poor.

This part of the Mass has also been known as the "Offertory," based on the Latin word *offerre*, which means to present, to bring, or to offer. Though it is now also called the Preparation of the Gifts, sacrificial themes remain. Indeed, there was much significance in the offering of these gifts, for they typically came from one's home or field and were made by one's hand. As such, they expressed a gift of one's self. Indeed, to part with the fruit of one's own hard labor would have had sacrificial overtones. This is why the presentation of the gifts symbolizes the individual's giving of himself to God.

---

[66] See CCC 1345.

# 13. The Presentation of the Gifts

The offering of bread and wine in the Mass has strong support in Scripture. In addition to being used in the Passover of Jesus' day and in the Last Supper (discussed later), bread and wine were offered up regularly in Israel's sacrificial rites. Consider the symbolism of bread and wine and what it would have meant to offer these gifts to God.

In the Bible, bread was not merely a side dish to a meal as it is in most Western societies today. For the ancient Israelites, bread was the most basic type of food, seen as necessary to sustain life (Sir 29:21; 39:26 [in some editions 39:31]). In fact, the expression "to eat bread" could describe simply eating in general (Gn 31:54; 37:25; 1 Kgs 13:8-9, 16-19). The Bible even depicts bread as similar to a staff ("the staff of bread"), which shows how bread was seen as a support for human life (Lv 26:26; Ps 105:16; Ez 4:16; 5:16). Yet the Israelites were called to give up some of their bread in the regular offerings and sacrifices (Ex 29:2; Lv 2:4-7; 7:13) and in the annual Feast of Weeks ceremony (Lv 23:15-20). To part with one's bread would have been a personal sacrifice, expressing the individual's giving of himself to God.

Similarly, wine was not just a side beverage, but a common part of the ancient Israelite meals. It was often consumed with bread (Jgs 19:19; 1 Sam 16:20; Ps 104:15; Jgs 10:5) and was served at feasts (1 Sam 25:36; Job 1:13) and for guests (Gn 14:18). Yet, like bread, wine was also offered up in Israel's sacrifices. It was one of the first fruits presented to the Temple as a tithe (Neh 10:36-39), and it was poured out as a drink offering (a libation) in Israel's thanksgiving and expiatory sacrifices (Ex 29:38-41; Nm 15:2-15). Since there was a close connection between the sacrificial gifts and the individual giver, offering bread and wine symbolized the offering of one's self.

The same is true with the presentation of our gifts in the Mass today. In the bread and wine, we offer back to God the gifts of creation and the result of our labors—or as the prayer in the Mass calls them, "fruit of the earth and work of human hands." Ultimately, the rite symbolizes our giving of our entire lives to God in the offering of bread and wine. As one commentator noted, "There is no scrap of bread which does not call to mind the hard work of plowing and sowing, the moist brow of the reaper, the weariness of the arms which have threshed the corn, and the grunts of the baker who kneaded the dough close to the scorching oven."[67] The same could be said of the wine, which comes from the grapes which were harvested from the vines that had been carefully tended throughout the year.

### More than Money

The practice of giving money (which eventually overshadowed the offering of oil, flax, and other sundry gifts) can be seen in the same light. Putting money in the basket is not simply a contribution to some good cause. It, too, expresses the giving of our lives to God. Our money embodies hours of our lives and hard work, which we now offer to God during Mass in the presentation of the gifts.

Yet, some Christians might wonder, "Why does God need our gifts? He sent his Son to die for our sins. Why does he need our meager sacrifices of bread, wine, and money?" Ultimately, God

---

[67] Georges Chevrot, *Our Mass* (Collegeville, MN: The Liturgical Press, 1958), p. 98.

does not need these things. Lacking nothing, God is God with or without our gifts. But *we* need to grow in self-giving love, and this is one reason why he invites us to unite our lives to him in this way. These small offerings help us to grow in sacrificial love. Moreover, though they do not count for much on their own, what gives them immense value is that we unite them with Christ's perfect sacrifice. In the presentation of the gifts, it is as if we bring our entire lives and all our little sacrifices (which are symbolized by the gifts) to the hands of Jesus Himself (who is represented by the priest).[68] The priest then brings our gifts to the altar, which is the place where Christ's sacrifice is made present, in order to express our union with Christ's offering to the Father.

---

[68]   See Jeremy Driscoll, *What Happens at Mass*, p. 66.

## 14. Mixing Water and Wine, Washing Hands, and Prayer over the Offerings

Though it was a common practice in the ancient world to dilute wine with a bit of water, Christians have seen profound theological significance in the mixing of water and wine at this moment in the liturgy. The meaning is expressed in the prayer that accompanies this rite: "By the mystery of this water and wine may we come to share in the divinity of Christ, who humbled himself to share in our humanity." In a traditional interpretation of this practice, the wine symbolizes Christ's divinity and water symbolizes our humanity. The mingling of the water and wine points to the Incarnation: the mystery of God becoming man. It also points to our call to share in Christ's divine life, to become "partakers of the divine nature" (2 Pt 1:4).

The priest also prays over the bread and wine, using words which have roots in Jewish tradition. They are modeled after the Jewish blessings over bread and wine used in meals probably around the time of Jesus:

> "Blessed are you, Lord God of all creation,
> for through your goodness we have received
> the bread we offer you:
> fruit of the earth and work of human hands,
> it will become for us the bread of life."

*"Blessed are you, Lord God of all creation,*
*for through your goodness we have received*
*the wine offered you:*
*fruit of the vine and work of human hands*
*it will become our spiritual drink."*

## May *We* Be Accepted by You

The priest's next prayer makes even clearer the connection between the gifts of bread and wine and the giver who offers them to God. The priest prays, "With humble spirit and contrite heart may we be accepted by you, O Lord, and may our sacrifice in your sight this day be pleasing to you, Lord God." Notice how the sacrifice envisioned in this prayer is not some *thing* being offered to God, like bread and wine, but the people assembled: "May *we* be accepted by you ..."

This theme, as well as the mention of a humble spirit and contrite heart, recalls the petition of the three Hebrew men thrown in the fiery furnace in Daniel 3. Being persecuted by the Babylonian king, Shadrach, Meschach, and Abednego cried out to God with a "humble spirit" and a "contrite heart" asking that they themselves would be accepted by the Lord just as a burnt offering in the temple would. In other words, the three men associated *their very lives* with a sacrifice offered up to God (Dn 3:15-16 [RSV–CE]; 3:39-40 [NAB]). The Lord heard their cry and rescued them. At Mass, the priest makes a similar petition. We have seen how our lives are bound up with the bread and wine offered to the Lord. Now the priest—like Shadrach, Meschach, and Abednego—cries out on our behalf to God with a "humble spirit" and a "contrite heart," asking that we be accepted as a pleasing sacrifice.

## Entering the Holy of Holies

Next, the priest washes his hands in a gesture that signals a dramatic event is about to take place. This practice recalls rites for the priests of the Old Testament. At their consecration, the priests and

Levites had to undergo ritual washings before they could perform their duties in the sanctuary (Ex 29:4; Nm 8:7). The priests needed to wash their hands (and feet) in a bronze basin of water before entering the tabernacle or drawing near to the altar of incense (Ex 30:17-21). Psalm 24 reflects the importance of this ritual for people preparing to enter the Temple: "Who shall ascend the hill of the Lord? And who shall stand in his holy place? He who has clean hands and a pure heart" (Ps 24:3-4). Notice how clean hands are associated with a pure heart. In this psalm, ritual hand-washing symbolizes the internal cleansing of heart required before a person could draw near to God's presence in the sanctuary.

With this biblical background, we can see that the priest's hand-washing at Mass indicates that he, like the Levitical priests of old, is about to stand in a most holy place—one that is even more awe-inspiring than the tabernacle or temple. God's presence sometimes manifested itself visibly in the form of a cloud in the Old Testament sanctuaries (Ex 40:34; 1 Kgs 8:10-11). But in the Mass, God is about to come to his people in an even more intimate way. On the altar before which the priest stands, the gifts of bread and wine will soon be changed into Christ's very body and blood, and Our Lord will soon dwell within us as we receive him in holy communion. Jesus, the one true High Priest, will accomplish this through the priest's hands. In preparation for this most sacred moment, the priest washes his hands like the priests of old as he approaches a new "the holy of holies." And he echoes David's humble prayer of contrition to prepare his soul for this holy task: "Wash me, O Lord, from my iniquity and cleanse me from my sin" (see Ps 51:2).

The congregation sits silently in awe as they watch the priest prepare for his sacred role in word and ritual. Finally, in one last act of preparation, the priest turns to the people, begging them for prayers as he is about to begin the Eucharistic prayer:

> *"Pray, brethren,*
> *that my sacrifice and yours*

*may be acceptable to God,*
*the almighty Father."*

The new translation of this prayer more accurately reflects the original Latin text of the Mass which refers to "my" sacrifice and "yours" and brings the meaning of this prayer out more beautifully. The "my" part of the sacrifice points to Christ's sacrifice which will be made present through the ordained priest who acts *in persona Christi* ("in the person of Christ"). The "your" part of the sacrifice refers to the entire Church offering itself in union with Christ in the Mass. The people respond with a prayer that recognizes how both sacrifices—Christ's and their own—will be united and offered to the Father through the *hands* of the priest:[69]

> *"May the Lord accept the sacrifice at your hands*
> *for the praise and glory of his name*
> *for our good and the good of all his holy Church."*

---

[69] The faithful at Mass offer the sacrifice "not only by the hands of the priest, but also, to a certain extent, in union with him" (Pius XII, *Mediator Dei*, no. 92). This is the laity's fullest participation in Christ's priesthood.

# B. The Eucharistic Prayer

Scholars have noted that the Eucharistic prayer has roots in Jewish table prayers recited at every meal. Near the start of the meal, the father of the family or the one presiding over the community would take bread and speak a blessing (*barakah*) which praised God, saying: "Blessed are you, Lord, our God, king of the universe, who has brought forth bread from heaven." The bread was then broken and given to the participants, and the people began eating the various courses of the meal. In the Passover meal, there also would be a reading of the *haggadah*, which re-told the story of the first Passover in Egypt and interpreted that foundational event in Israel's history for the current generation. This made God's saving deeds of the past present and applied the story to their lives.

When the meal neared its conclusion, the presider prayed a second and longer *barakah* over a cup of wine. This blessing had three parts: 1) *praise* of God for his creation; 2) *thanksgiving* for his redemptive work in the past (for example, the giving of the covenant, the land, the law); and 3) *supplication* for the future, that God's saving works would continue in their lives and be brought to their climax in the sending of the Messiah who would restore the Davidic kingdom.

The early Eucharistic prayers seem to have followed this general pattern. They included reciting a blessing over bread and wine, re-telling the foundational saving event of Jesus' death and resurrection, and the three-fold structure of offering *praise* to God for creation, *thanksgiving* for his saving deeds and *supplication*. And as we will soon see, these ancient Jewish elements are also found in the Eucharistic prayers of the Mass today.

We will now consider the following parts of the Eucharistic prayer: 1) the Preface; 2) the *Sanctus*; 3) the *Epiclesis*; 4) the Words of Institution/Consecration; 5) the "Mystery of Faith"; and 6) the *Anamanesis*, Offering, Intercessions, and Doxology.

# 15. The Preface

The Eucharistic Prayer opens with a three-part dialogue that
has been recited in the Church since at least the third century:

> *Priest:* The Lord be with you.
> *People:* And with your spirit.
>
> *Priest:* Lift up your hearts.
> *People:* We lift them up to the Lord.
>
> *Priest:* Let us give thanks to the Lord our God.
> *People:* It is right and just.

This dialogue is first reported in the Eucharistic prayer of
St. Hippolytus (c. A.D. 215). Now, eighteen centuries later, we
continue to say the same words, uniting us with the Christians of
the early Church.

## The Lord be with you

The opening exchange ("The Lord be with you...And with
your spirit") we have heard before. It was used in the Introductory
Rites at the start of Mass and just before the reading of the Gospel.
In Chapter 2, we saw that, in the Bible, greetings like this were used
to address those whom God called to an important but daunting

mission. They needed the Lord to be with them as they set out on their charge. Here, the greeting is fittingly repeated as we embark upon the most sacred part of the Mass: the Eucharistic prayer. Both the priest and the people need the Lord to be with them as they prepare to enter into the mystery of the holy sacrifice of the Mass.

## Lifting Our Hearts

Next, the priest says, "Lift up your hearts" (*Sursum corda* in Latin). This prayer brings to mind the similar exhortation in the book of Lamentations: "Let us lift up our hearts and hands to God in heaven" (Lam 3:41). But what does it mean to "lift up" our hearts?

In the Bible, the heart is the hidden center of the person from which one's thoughts, emotions and actions originate. All intentions and commitments flow from the human heart. Therefore, when the priest at Mass says "Lift up your hearts," he is summoning us to give our fullest attention to what is about to unfold. This is a "wake-up call" to set aside all other concerns and focus our minds, wills and emotions—our hearts—on the sublimity of what is happening in the Eucharistic prayer.

This summons is reminiscent of St. Paul's words to the Colossians: "If then you have been raised with Christ, seek the things that are above, where Christ is, seated at the right hand of God. *Set your minds on things that are above*, not on things that are on earth" (Col 3:1-2). Just as Paul called the Colossians to seek the "things that are above, *where Christ is*," so are we bidden to direct our entire being toward the things of heaven, for that is where Christ is. And that is where we are going in the Eucharistic prayer.

## Our Fullest Attention

St. Cyprian (d. A.D. 258), a North African Church Father, explained how this prayer draws our attention away from worldly distractions and is meant to lead us to ponder the awe-inspiring action taking place in the Eucharistic prayer:

> When we stand praying, beloved brethren, we ought to be watchful and earnest with our whole heart, intent on our prayers. Let all carnal and worldly thoughts pass away, nor let the soul at that time think on anything but the object only of its prayer. For this reason also the priest by way of preface before his prayer, prepares the minds of the brethren by saying, *Lift up your hearts,* that so upon the people's response, *We have them before our Lord,* he may be reminded that he himself ought to think of nothing but our Lord.[70]

Another Church Father, St. Cyril of Jerusalem, made a similar point and warned believers of the seriousness of this moment.

> *Lift up your hearts:* For in this sublime moment the heart should be lifted up to God, and not be allowed to descend to the earth and to earthly concerns. With all possible emphasis the sacrificing priest exhorts us in this hour to lay aside all the cares of this life, all domestic worries, and direct our hearts to God in heaven who hath so loved men.... Let there be none among you, who shall confess with his lips: We have lifted up our hearts, and allow his thoughts to remain with the cares of this life.[71]

Cyril goes on to acknowledge that being attentive to the Lord is something we should do always, but is difficult because we are fallen and weak. Yet, if there ever is a moment to concentrate

---

[70] St. Cyprian, *De dominica oratione*, c. 31. As translated in Thomas Crean, *The Mass and the Saints*, pp. 93-4.

[71] St. Cyril of Jerusalem, *Cat. Myst.,* 5, 4-5. As translated in Pius Parsch, *The Liturgy of the Mass*, p. 216.

most intently and give God our fullest attention, it is now at the Eucharistic prayer: "We should, indeed think of God at all times, but this is impossible because of our human frailty; but in this holy time especially our hearts should be with God."[72]

## The Great Thanksgiving

In the last liturgical exchange, the priest says "Let us give thanks to the Lord our God...." As we already have seen in the *Gloria* ("We give you thanks...") and in the response to the Scripture readings ("Thanks be to God"), thanksgiving is a common biblical response to God's goodness and to his saving works in our lives. The priest directing us to give thanks to the Lord echoes the similar exhortation found in the Psalms: "Give thanks to the Lord for he is good..." (Ps 136:1-3; see also Ps 107:8, 15, 21, 31). In the Jewish tradition, thanksgiving is one thing we can actually offer the Creator that he does not possess already. The first century Jewish commentator Philo expressed this point:

> We affirm that the activity most characteristic of God is to give His blessings. But that most fitting to creation is to give thanks, because that is the best it can offer him in return. For when creation tries to make any other return to God it finds that its gift already belongs to the Creator of the universe, not to the creature offering it. Since we now realize that to give due worship to God only one duty is incumbent upon us, that of giving thanks, we must carry it out in all times and in all places.[73]

St. Paul similarly teaches that the Christian life should be marked by prayers of thanksgiving. We should be "abounding in thanksgiving" (Col 2:7), giving thanks to God in all we do (Col

---

[72]  Ibid.

[73]  Philo, *De Plantatione*, 130-31, as translated in A.G. Martimort, *The Signs of the New Covenant* (Collegeville, MN: Liturgical Press, 1963), p. 169.

3:17) and "in all circumstances" (1 Thess 5:18; cf. Phil 4:6), especially in worship (see 1 Cor 14:16-19; Eph 5:19-20; Col 3:16).

Following this biblical tradition of offering prayers of thanksgiving, the priest invites us to "give thanks to the Lord our God." And there is a lot to be thankful for at this point in the Mass. Like the ancient Israelites who thanked the Lord for delivering them from their enemies, so we now should thank God for sending his Son to save us from sin and the Evil One. That redemptive act of Christ's death and resurrection is about to be made present to us in the liturgy, and we humbly express our gratitude.

We also should be thankful for the miracle about to take place in our midst, as the bread and wine on the altar will be changed into the body and blood of Jesus. Our Lord and King will soon be with us in the Real Presence of the Eucharist. Our hearts should be filled with gratitude as our church becomes like a new holy of holies, housing the divine presence. What an awesome privilege it is for us to draw near! We are like the ancient Israelites who approached the temple of God's dwelling with joyous psalms of praise and thanksgiving. In fact, we should hear in the priest's instruction, "Let us give thanks to the Lord our God," an echo of the Psalmist's words to those pilgrims as they drew near to Jerusalem: "Let us come into his presence with thanksgiving" (Ps 95:2) or "Enter his gates with thanksgiving" (Ps 100:4).

There is so much to be thankful for at this moment in the Liturgy! We therefore acknowledge that gratitude is the only fitting response to the mysteries about to unfold before us. In answer to the priest's invitation to thank the Lord, we say, "It is right and just."

## Preface Prayer

After inviting us to give thanks to the Lord, the priest now talks to God in a prayer of thanksgiving. The opening line is addressed to the Father and expresses what we have seen throughout Scripture: the duty of God's people to thank the Lord. One option for the

Preface prayer, for example, begins, "It is truly right and just, our duty and salvation, always and everywhere to give you thanks, Father most holy...." But the priest does not say this prayer for himself. He offers it on behalf of the people who just expressed their desire to join the priest in thanking God when they said that "It is right and just" to give God thanks and praise. St. John Chrysostom made this point, noting how the priest (envisioned by Chrysostom as the bishop) represents the people in this prayer: "The prayer of thanksgiving is made in common. The bishop does not give thanks alone, but the whole assembly joins him. For, though the bishop speaks for the people, he does so only after they have said that it is fitting and right that he should begin the Eucharist."[74]

This Preface prayer follows the pattern of thanksgiving in the psalms in the Old Testament. Thanksgiving in general was offered for the gift of God's creation (Ps 136:4-9), for his provision in their lives (Ps 67:6-7), for his wondrous deeds (Ps 75:1) and for his saving acts (Ps 35:18). In these kinds of psalms, God's people responded with gratitude for the Lord rescuing a person in a particular way, whether it be healing (Ps 30, 116), saving someone from their enemies (Ps 18, 92, 118, 138) or delivering them from some trouble (66:14). The psalmist gives an account of his trials and how God rescued him, which serves as the basis for the praise and thanksgiving.

This pattern can be seen in Psalm 136, which starts with the Psalmist thanking God for his marvelous works of creation: for making the earth, the waters, the stars, the sun, and the moon (Ps 136:4-9). The Psalm then moves to recount God's saving deeds in Israel's history: bringing them out of Egypt, parting the Red Sea, overthrowing Pharaoh in the waters, leading them through the wilderness and defeating Israel's enemies. Next, the Psalmist proclaims how this same God, who rescued their ancestors long ago, has also performed an act of deliverance for God's people in the

---

[74] St. John Chrysostom, *Homily* on 2 Corinthians 18:3, as translated in A.G. Martimort, *The Signs of the New Covenant*, p. 170.

present. This same God who delivered their ancestors from Egypt has also "remembered *us* in our low estate" and "rescued *us* from our foes" (Ps 136:23-24). Therefore, the community gathered with the Psalmist has great cause for thanksgiving. God's love for his people has been steadfast throughout history. He has been faithful to his people from the time of the Exodus to the present. The Psalmist thus concludes, "O give thanks to the God of heaven, for his steadfast love endures forever" (Ps 136:26).

The Eucharistic prayers follow this biblical pattern. For we, like the psalmists of old, have much to be thankful for. Like Psalm 136, the Eucharistic prayer recounts God's marvelous deeds in salvation history. This recounting may take on various forms, as there are several options for the preface. Some forms of this prayer thank God for his work of creation. Others highlight specific aspects of Christ's saving work, depending on the feast or season. For example, in the Christmas season, the priest thanks God for becoming man. In Holy Week, the priest refers to how the hour is approaching when Jesus triumphed over Satan. In the Easter Season, the priest thanks God for the eternal life Christ has won for us. But all these prayers focus on thanking God for the very heart of his saving plan: Christ's life-giving death and resurrection.

# 16. The *Sanctus*: "Holy, Holy, Holy Lord"

*"Holy, Holy, Holy Lord God of hosts.*
*Heaven and earth are full of your glory.*
  *Hosanna in the highest.*
*Blessed is he who comes in the name of the Lord.*
  *Hosanna in the highest."*

This prayer helps us to see with the eyes of the angels what is really happening in the Eucharistic liturgy. Right away, the opening words "Holy, holy, holy Lord…" take us spiritually up to heaven. They come from Isaiah 6:3, a passage in which the prophet receives a vision of the heavenly King in the divine throne room with his majesty magnificently displayed and his angelic court adoring him.

Isaiah reports that he saw "the Lord sitting upon a throne, high and lifted up; and his train filled the temple" (Is 6:1). Above the Lord, Isaiah saw the six-winged angelic *seraphim*, a word which means "burning ones." This unique title suggests that these angels are so close to God that they reflect his radiance. Yet even these angelic beings stand in utter awe before the divine presence. They covered their faces, daring not to behold the full glory of God (Is 6:2), and called to one another in an ecstatic hymn of praise:

> *"Holy, holy, holy is the Lord of hosts;*
> *The whole earth is full of his glory." (Is 6:3)*

The three-fold repetition of the word "holy" here is the strongest form of the superlative in Hebrew. The seraphim, therefore, acclaim the Lord as the all-holy One, the one God above all other gods. And by singing "the whole earth is full of his glory," they praise God for his splendor, which is displayed throughout creation (see Ps 8:1; 19:1-6; 24:1-3).

This angelic hymn of praise has dramatic effects. When they sing, the foundations of the Temple shake and the room is filled with smoke. Isaiah understandably feels afraid. Recognizing his unworthiness to stand in the holy presence of God, he says, "Woe is me! For I am lost; for I am a man of unclean lips...for my eyes have seen the King, the Lord of hosts!" (Is 6:5).

## Singing with the Angels

In the New Testament, St. John had a similar experience. He was caught up in the Spirit on the Lord's day (Rv 1:10) and had an ecstatic vision of the heavenly liturgy. John sees Jesus, the Son of Man, in radiant glory, and like Isaiah he responds in fear: "When I saw him, I fell at his feet as though dead" (Rv 1:17). Again, like Isaiah, John sees the six-winged angelic creatures before the throne of God who sing a similar hymn of praise: "Holy, holy, holy, is the Lord God Almighty, who was and is and is to come" (Rv 4:8). Reminiscent of Isaiah's account of the seraphim praising God for his glory revealed in the cosmos, John reports how "the twenty-four elders" fall down before God's throne praising him for his creation as they sing:

> *"Worthy art though, our Lord and God,*
> *to receive glory and honor and power,*
> *for thou didst create all things,*
> *and by thy will they existed and were created." (Rv 4:11)*

With this background in mind, we can understand more clearly what it means for us to say at Mass: "Holy, holy, holy Lord, God of hosts..." We are joining our voices with the angels and saints in heaven in their jubilant hymn of praise. And how fitting it is to do so at this very moment in the Mass! In the Eucharistic liturgy, we become like Isaiah and St. John, caught up to the heavenly liturgy.[75] We are mystically entering the heavenly throne room—the same one that Isaiah saw in his earth-shaking vision that filled the Temple with smoke as the angels sang. Both the prophet and the apostle felt unworthy to behold this awesome sign, and even the seraphim felt the need to cover their faces as they flew before the glory of God. Like them, we are preparing to encounter the King of Kings, the all-holy divine Lord, who will become present on the altar. No wonder we fall to our knees in reverence after singing this hymn.

In the second half of this prayer known as the *Sanctus* (Latin for "holy"), we repeat words which the crowds used to greet Jesus as He processed into Jerusalem: "Hosanna" and "Blessed is he who comes in the name of the Lord." Both expressions were originally in Psalm 118, a pilgrimage hymn recited on the way to the Temple for major feasts. *Hosanna* is a transliteration of a Hebrew word meaning "Save us," which became an expression of praise in liturgical worship. The blessing upon "he who comes in the name of the Lord" was normally invoked on the pilgrims coming to the Temple. On the day we know as Palm Sunday, the crowds used these words to welcome Jesus as the one coming in the Lord's name—in other words, the one representing God and acting on his behalf.

It is fitting that we repeat these words at this moment in the Liturgy. Just as the crowds in Jerusalem welcomed Jesus into the holy city with these words from Psalm 118, so do we welcome Jesus into our churches, for he is about to become present in the Eucharist on our altars.

---

[75]  See CCC 1139.

# 17. The *Epiclesis*

We saw earlier that in the ancient Jewish table prayers, the blessing over the cup included a supplication that God send the Messiah to Israel and restore the Davidic Kingdom. Quite naturally, the early Christians included in the Eucharistic prayer a similar supplication. In a prayer known as the *epiclesis* (meaning "invocation upon"), the priest prays that the Father send the Holy Spirit so that the gifts of bread and wine be changed into the body and blood of Our Lord. Like the ancient Jews who pleaded with God to send the Messiah, the priest at Mass petitions that the Messiah-King be made present once again, this time under the appearances of bread and wine: "Make holy, therefore, these gifts, we pray, by sending down your Spirit upon them like the dewfall, so that they may become for us the Body and Blood of our Lord, Jesus Christ" (Eucharistic Prayer II); or "Therefore, O Lord, we humbly implore you: by the same Spirit graciously make holy these gifts we have brought to you for consecration, that they may become the body and blood of your Son our Lord Jesus Christ" (Eucharistic Prayer III).

There is a second epiclesis after the words of institution that relates to the other petition made in the ancient Jewish prayers, that of the House of David being restored. Just as many Jews expected the Messiah to unite God's people in a restored Davidic kingdom, so we confidently hope that the Messiah who comes to us in the Eucharist will unite us more deeply together in his Church. Hence, the priest calls on the Holy Spirit, praying that the Eucharist may draw all those who receive into a greater communion: "Grant that we, who are nourished by the Body and Blood of your Son and filled with his Holy Spirit, *may become one body, one spirit in Christ*" (Eucharistic Prayer III; emphasis added). Similarly, in other Eucharistic Prayers, the priest petitions that after receiving the one Body of Christ in the Eucharist, "we may be gathered into one" (Eucharistic Prayer III) or "gathered into one body" (Eucharistic Prayer IV).

## 18. The Words of Institution and Consecration

*"TAKE THIS, ALL OF YOU, AND EAT OF IT,*
  *FOR THIS IS MY BODY,*
  *WHICH WILL BE GIVEN UP FOR YOU...*
*TAKE THIS, ALL OF YOU, AND DRINK FROM IT,*
  *FOR THIS IS THE CHALICE OF MY BLOOD,*
  *THE BLOOD OF THE NEW AND ETERNAL COVENANT,*
  *WHICH WILL BE POURED OUT FOR YOU AND FOR MANY*
  *FOR THE FORGIVENESS OF SINS.*
  *DO THIS IN MEMORY OF ME."*

For some Catholics, these words might be *too* familiar. Some of us have heard these words hundreds of times since our childhood repeated at every Mass. We might be tempted to take them for granted or consider them routine.

But what if we had never heard these words before? What if we were Peter, James, or one of the other apostles present at the Last Supper? What would these words have meant to us?

In order to understand the full meaning of these sacred words, it is important to hear them against the background of the Passover. The gospels that recount the institution narrative tell us that the Last Supper took place in the context of the Passover meal—the annual feast that celebrated the foundational night in Israel's history when God liberated them from Egypt (Mt 26:19; Mk 14:16; Lk 22:13). On that first Passover, God instructed the people to sacrifice an unblemished lamb, eat of the lamb, and mark their doorposts with the blood of the lamb. The families who participated in this ritual were spared when the firstborn sons in Egypt were struck down in the tenth plague. Year after year, subsequent Israelites re-told the story of that first Passover and re-enacted it, eating a sacrificial lamb once again.

Most significantly, the Israelites celebrated the annual Passover (see Ex 12:14) as a liturgical "memorial" (*anamnesis* in Greek). For the ancient Jews, this involved much more than remembering a past event. A memorial such as Passover was very different from modern holidays such as the Fourth of July, on which Americans simply call to mind the founding of their country. In a biblical "memorial," the past was not merely recalled; it was *re-lived*. The past event was mystically made present to those celebrating the feast. This is why Jews in Jesus' day believed that when they celebrated this feast, the first Passover was made present to them as a "memorial." In fact, when later Jewish rabbis wrote about the Passover, they said that when a Jew celebrates the feast, it was as if he himself were walking out of Egypt with his great ancestors from the Exodus generation.[76] The *Catechism of the Catholic Church* makes a similar point:

> In the sense of Sacred Scripture the *memorial* is not merely the recollection of past events but the proclamation of the mighty works wrought by God for men. In the liturgical celebration of these events, they become in a certain way present and real. This is how Israel understands its liberation from Egypt: every time Passover is celebrated, the Exodus events are made present to the memory of believers so that they may conform their lives to them.[77]

---

[76] *Pesahim*, 10.5.
[77] CCC 1363.

In this way, the first Passover event was extended in time so that each new generation could participate spiritually in this foundational event of their liberation from servitude. The annual Passover feast thus forged solidarity throughout the generations. All Israelites participated in the Passover. All were saved from slavery in Egypt. All were united in the one covenant family of God.

## The Mass as Sacrifice?

If you were one of the apostles present at the Last Supper, one thing that might strike you about Jesus' words is that he used sacrificial language with reference to Himself. First, the Passover itself was a sacrifice (Ex 12:27). For Jesus to speak about body and blood in the context of Passover would bring to mind the Passover lamb, the blood of which was separated from the body in the ceremonial sacrifice. Second, when Jesus says his body "will be *given up for you*," the term used in Luke's gospel for "given up" (*didomai* in Greek) is significant, for it is employed elsewhere in the New Testament in association with sacrifice (see, for example, Lk 2:24; Mk 10:45; Jn 6:51; Gal 1:4). Third, when Jesus speaks of his blood "which will be poured out…for the forgiveness of sins," he alludes to the atoning sacrifices in the Temple, which involved blood being poured out over the altar for the purpose of bringing forgiveness (see Lv 4:7, 18, 25, 30, 34).

Fourth, and perhaps most significantly, Jesus speaks of "the blood of the new and eternal covenant." These words echo what Moses said in the sacrificial ceremony at Mount Sinai that sealed God's covenant union with Israel as his chosen people (Ex 24:1-17). In the midst of that sacrificial rite, Moses took the blood of the animals and announced, "Behold the blood of the covenant" (Ex 24:8). Now, at the Last Supper, Jesus refers to *his* blood as "the blood of the new and eternal covenant." For the apostles present there, these words could not help but recall what Moses said about the sacrificial blood at Sinai and point to some kind of new sacrifice for a new covenant.

With all these sacrificial themes—the Passover ritual, a body being given up, blood being poured out, and the blood of the covenant—Jesus clearly has some type of sacrifice in mind here. Yet, instead of speaking about the Passover lamb being sacrificed (which is what one might expect in the context of a Passover meal), he talks about *his own* body and blood being offered up and poured out in sacrifice. *His* blood is now the sacrificial blood of the covenant. Jesus surprisingly identifies *himself* with the sacrificial lamb normally offered for Passover. As such, Jesus' actions at the Last Supper mysteriously anticipate his sacrifice on the cross. In the Passover meal of the Last Supper, Jesus willingly offers up his own body and blood for the forgiveness of sins. All that was left for him to do was to carry out that sacrifice in a bloody manner on Good Friday.[78]

Understanding this connection between the Last Supper and the cross will shed important light on how the Eucharist we celebrate today commemorates Christ's sacrifice on Calvary. For Jesus concludes the institution of the Eucharist by saying, "Do this in memory of me." What is the "this" that Jesus commands the apostles to do? Celebrate the New Passover sacrifice of his body and blood. And how are they to do it? As a biblical memorial. The word "memory" used in the Mass translates the biblical word for "memorial" (*anamnesis*), which, as we have seen, means much more than merely remembering the past. A liturgical memorial brings the past and present together, making the long-ago event mystically present for the current generation. Hence, when Jesus commands the apostles, "Do this in memory of me," he is not telling them to perform a simple ritual meal that will help people remember him.

---

[78] "Jesus did not simply state that what he was giving them to eat and drink was his body and blood; he also expressed its *sacrificial meaning* and made sacramentally present his sacrifice which would soon be offered on the Cross for the salvation of all" (John Paul II, *Ecclesia de Eucharistia*, no. 12).

He is instructing them to celebrate the Last Supper as a liturgical memorial. All that was involved with the Last Supper—most particularly, the sacrificial offering of Christ's body and blood—would be made present to worshipers in the celebration of the Eucharist.

Therefore, as the memorial of the Lord's Supper, the Eucharist makes the events of the Upper Room and Calvary sacramentally present to us today. Just as the ancient Jews year-after-year participated in the Exodus through the memorial of Passover, so do we Christians participate in the new Exodus of Jesus' triumphant death on the cross every time we celebrate the new Passover of the Eucharist.

It is in this sense that the Mass is to be understood as a sacrifice. As the *Catechism* explains, "In the New Testament, the memorial takes on new meaning. When the Church celebrates the Eucharist, she commemorates Christ's Passover, and it is made present: the sacrifice Christ offered once for all on the cross remains ever present."[79] And this sacrifice is made present for a salvific purpose: so that its power may be applied to our lives for the daily sins we commit and so that we can unite ourselves more deeply to Christ in his act of total self-giving love.[80]

Indeed, in every Mass, we have a unique opportunity to enter sacramentally into the Son's intimate, loving gift of himself to the Father—a gift that is revealed most clearly in his death on the cross. In the Mass, we can join all our joys and sufferings with Jesus' offering of himself to the Father, and in so doing, we offer ever more of our own lives as a gift to the Father. As the *Catechism* explains, "In the Eucharist the sacrifice of Christ becomes also the sacrifice of the members of his Body. The lives of the faithful, their praise, sufferings, prayer, and work are united with those of Christ and with his total offering, and so acquire a new value. Christ's sacrifice pres-

---

[79] CCC 1364.
[80] See CCC 1366.

ent on the altar makes it possible for all generations of Christians to be united with his offering."[81]

## For Many or For All?

We conclude with brief notes on two changes in the new translation of the Mass. First, while the previous translation of the Words of Institution referred to "the cup" of Christ's blood, the new translation renders it "the chalice." This is a more faithful and more formal rendering of the Latin text of the Mass and one that underscores the liturgical nature of this vessel. This is no ordinary cup, but the Eucharistic cup (see Lk 22:20; 1 Cor 11:25ff.) that the Lord consecrated at the Last Supper. This most sacred of vessels has traditionally been called a "chalice," and so this is the term used in the new translation.

Second, the previous translation of the Mass referred to Jesus' blood having redemptive value "for all." But the new translation replaces the words "for all" with "for many":

> *"FOR THIS IS THE CHALICE OF MY BLOOD,*
> *THE BLOOD OF THE NEW AND ETERNAL COVENANT,*
> *WHICH WILL BE POURED OUT FOR YOU AND FOR MANY*
> *FOR THE FORGIVENESS OF SINS."*

This change in the translation remains closer to Jesus' actual words of institution in the gospels (Mt 26:28). It is also more harmonious with the Latin text of the Mass and with wording that has been used at this point in the liturgy for centuries. Some people have raised concerns, however, that the words "for many" limit the universal scope of Jesus' saving mission. It is feared that the new wording gives the impression that Jesus did not die on the cross for everyone—that he offered his blood on Calvary not "for all" but just for a select group of people ("for many").

However, on a basic level, the new translation points to the

---

[81]  CCC 1368.

reality that while Jesus died for all, not everyone chooses to accept this gift. Each individual must choose to welcome the gift of salvation and live according to this grace, so that he or she may be among "the many" who are described in this text.

Moreover, many Scripture scholars have observed that Jesus' language at the Last Supper about his blood being poured out "for many" recalls "the many" that are three times mentioned in Isaiah 53:11-12.[82] In this prophecy, Isaiah foretold that God one day would send his servant who would make himself "an offering for sin," pouring out his soul to death and bearing the sin of "many" and making "many" righteous (Is 53:10-12). Jesus, speaking at the Last Supper about his own blood being poured out "for many," is clearly associating himself with the Suffering Servant of Isaiah. He is the one coming to die for the "many." This should not be understood, however, in opposition to the fact that Jesus died "for all" (1 Tm 2:6). The other prophecies in Isaiah about the Servant of the Lord make clear that he has a universal mission, one that announces salvation to *all* humanity (see, for example, Is 42:1-10; 49:6; 52:10). In a sense, the expression "the many" can be seen as contrasting the *one* person who dies—the Lord's Servant (Jesus)—with *the many* who benefit from his atoning sacrifice.

---

[82] The Greek Septuagint translation of the Old Testament uses the word *polloi* ('many') three times in these verses.

# 19. The "Mystery of Faith"

W e have arrived at the supreme moment of the Mass. The priest has spoken the words of consecration over the bread and wine, and they have now become the body and blood of Christ. In reverence, the priest genuflects in silent adoration before Christ's Blood in the chalice and then rises and solemnly says, "The mystery of faith."

These words are not so much a ceremonial instruction for the people to say their part next. Rather, they express the priest's profound wonder and awe over the mystery that is taking place. Jesus Christ, the Son of God, whose body and blood were offered for our sins on Calvary, is now really present on the altar under the appearances of bread and wine. Using an expression of St. Paul (1 Tm 3:9), the priest exclaims that this truly is "the mystery of faith"!

Joining the priest's wonder over this mystery, the people proclaim the story of salvation summed up in Jesus' death and resurrection. Two of the acclamations options draw from St. Paul's words to the Corinthians: "For as often as you eat this bread and drink this cup, you proclaim the Lord's death until he comes" (1 Cor 11:26):

> *"We proclaim your Death, O Lord,*
> *and profess your Resurrection*
> *until you come again."*

OR

> "When we eat this Bread and drink this Cup,
> we proclaim your Death, O Lord,
> until you come again."

A third option proclaims the saving power of Christ's death and resurrection while drawing on the words of the Samaritans who, after encountering Jesus, came to believe in him, saying, "We know that this is indeed the Savior of the world" (Jn 4:42).

> "Save us, Savior of the world,
> for by your Cross and Resurrection
> you have set us free."

# 20. The *Anamnesis*, Offering, Intercessions, and the Final Doxology

The ineffable mysteries unfolding before us cannot be taken in all at once. It is as if we need to pause and lengthen the moment in order to grasp their meaning and enter into them. The next two prayers following the words of institution do just that; they make explicit various aspects of what is happening in the liturgy and allow us to ponder them in our hearts.

The first prayer is called the *anamnesis*. We have seen how the whole Eucharistic prayer is a "memorial" (or *anamnesis* in Greek), making present Christ's saving action on the cross so that we might participate in its power more fully. In a stricter, more technical sense, however, the *anamnesis* refers to a prayer which identifies what is happening in the Mass. Jesus said, "Do this in memory of me." Now, the priest tells the Father in heaven that the Church has been faithful in fulfilling this command:

> *"Therefore, as we celebrate the memorial of his Death and Resurrection..."* (Eucharistic Prayer II)

God, of course, does not need to be informed of our liturgical actions; He knows of them already and understands their meaning perfectly. We, however, have a need to tell him. Like small children who eagerly tell their parents their accomplishments ("Dad, did you see me hit the ball into the outfield? I made it all the way to second base!"), we have a need to tell our heavenly Father of our joyous participation in these sacred mysteries.

## Offering

The *anamnesis* serves as the basis for a second prayer known as "the offering," which expresses how in the Mass we have the awesome privilege of offering what Jesus offered on Good Friday. On the cross, Jesus offered up his sacrifice alone. In the Mass, he offers it with his Church as he associates us with this sacrifice.

> *"We offer you in thanksgiving this holy and living sacrifice."*
> (Eucharistic Prayer III)

As we saw above, we are invited to unite *ourselves* with this sacrifice of Christ, which is why the Eucharistic Prayer calls this not only Christ's sacrifice, but also "the oblation of your Church" (Eucharistic Prayer III).   And the two are really one, since the Church at every Mass participates in the one self-giving act of Christ's offering on the cross.

The symbolism of the gifts also points to how the Church offers itself to God not on its own, but in union with Christ's sacrifice. Recall how the material gifts of bread and wine symbolized a total gift of one's very self. Now after the consecration, those human gifts to God have become the Eucharistic body and blood of Christ—the body and blood which is offered to the Father. Thus, in Christ, the Church participates in the perfect self-giving love of the Son on the cross. As the *General Instruction of the Roman Missal* explains:

> In this very memorial, the Church—and in particular
> the Church here and now gathered—offers in the Holy
> Spirit the spotless Victim to the Father. The Church's
> intention, however, is that the faithful not only offer
> this spotless Victim but also learn to offer themselves,
> and so day by day to be consummated, through Christ

the Mediator, into unity with God and with each other
so that at last God may be all in all.[83]

## Three Model Sacrifices

Eucharistic Prayer I goes on to cite three models of sacrifice
from the Bible, asking the Father to accept the Church's offering
as he was pleased to accept the sacrifices of Abel, Abraham, and
Melchizedek: "...accept them, as once you were pleased to accept
the gifts of your servant Abel the just, the sacrifice of Abraham, our
father in faith, and the offering of your high priest Melchizedek, a
holy sacrifice, a spotless victim."

Each of these Old Testament patriarchs made sacrifices that
prefigure Christ's and point to the kind of self-giving we should
offer God as we unite ourselves to his oblation.

God looked with favor on the sacrifice of the mysterious priest-
king, *Melchizedek*, who offered bread and wine to God and blessed
Abraham. From the earliest period of Christianity, his sacrifice has
been seen as prefiguring Christ's offering of bread and wine at the
Last Supper. The sacrifice of *Abel* reminds us to give our best to
God. In contrast to his brother Cain, who only gave the fruit from
the ground, Abel was willing to give the Lord his best, sacrificing
"the firstlings of his flock and of their fat portions" (Gn 4:4). God
had regard for Abel's generous sacrifice, but not for Cain's.

Finally, *Abraham* gave something more than bread, wine, or
animals. He was willing to offer God that which was most precious
to him: his own son, Isaac. And the events surrounding Abraham's
sacrifice prefigure Christ's sacrifice on Calvary perhaps more than
any other sacrifice in the Old Testament. Genesis 22 tells how
Abraham took his only beloved son Isaac to Mount Moriah on a
donkey. Isaac carried the wood for the sacrifice up the mountain
and was bound on the wood to be offered as a sacrifice for sin.
In response to this heroic act of total surrender, God swore that

---

[83]  *General Instruction of the Roman Missal, Third Typical Edition*, no. 79.

he would bless the whole human family through Abraham's descendants. Many centuries later, God the Father offers up his *only beloved son*, Jesus, in Jerusalem—a city associated with *Moriah*, the very place where Abraham offered up Isaac (see 2 Chr 3:1; Ps 76:2). Like Isaac, Jesus travels to this place on a *donkey*, and like Isaac, he *carries the wood* of the cross to Calvary. There, like Isaac again, Jesus is *bound* to the wood and offered as a *sacrifice* for sin—a sacrifice that brings about the *worldwide blessing* that God swore to Abraham in Genesis 22. On Good Friday, God the Father and God the Son, therefore, bring to fulfillment what was prefigured by Abraham and Isaac long ago, and God's oath to Abraham that he would bless the human family is realized.

### Intercessions

As the Eucharistic Prayers near their conclusion, the priest makes various intercessions. First, he prays for all who will soon be nourished by the body and blood of Christ. He prays that "they may become one body, one spirit in Christ" (Eucharistic Prayer III)—an echo of St. Paul's words in 1 Corinthians 10:17: "Because there is one bread, we who are many are one body, for we all partake of the one bread." The priest also prays that our participation in Christ's sacrifice might make us "an eternal offering to you"(Eucharistic Prayer III) or "a living sacrifice" (Eucharistic Prayer IV) echoing St. Paul's exhortation to the Romans: "Present your bodies as a living sacrifice, holy and acceptable to God, which is your spiritual worship" (Rom 12:1).

Second, the priest prays for the Church universal, naming the pope and the local bishop and then interceding for all bishops, clergy, and the entire people of God, both the living and the dead. Some intercessions include a universal scope, interceding for "all who seek you with a sincere heart" (Eucharistic Prayer IV) and praying that the sacrifice of the Mass "advance the peace and salvation of all the world" (Eucharistic Prayer III).

## The Doxology and the "Great Amen"

The Eucharistic Prayer culminates with an expression of praise that was used in the Mass as early as the second century. And the people respond with what is commonly known as "the great Amen"—and rightly so.

"Amen" transliterates a Hebrew word that affirms the validity of what has been said and was often used in liturgical settings. For example, when the Levites sang, "Blessed be the Lord, the God of Israel, from everlasting to everlasting," the people joined in this blessing of God by exclaiming, "Amen!" (1 Chr 16:36). When Ezra read the book of the law in a solemn ceremony, he concluded by blessing the Lord, and the people answered, "Amen, Amen" (Neh 8:6). St. Paul used this word in similar ways (Rom 1:25; Gal 1:5; Eph 3:21) and even concluded some of his letters with an "Amen" (1 Cor 16:24; also, in some manuscripts, 1 Thess 5:28; 2 Thess 3:18).

Most notable is how the angels and saints in heaven cry out "Amen" as they sing their part in the chorus praising God in the heavenly liturgy. In the book of Revelation, every living creature in heaven and earth and under the earth says, "To him who sits upon the throne and to the Lamb be blessing and honor and glory and might for ever and ever!" And in response, the angelic creatures say "Amen!" as if to shout out, "Yes! May the Lord be blessed and honored forever!" In another scene, the angels fall down in worship before God's throne, saying, "Amen! Blessing and glory and wisdom and thanksgiving and honor and power and might be to our God for ever and ever! Amen" (Rv 7:12; see also Rv 5:14; 19:4).

This praise of the angels and saints in heaven is echoed on earth by the priest at every Mass when he says,

> *Through him, and with him, and in him,*
> *O God, almighty Father, in the unity of the Holy Sprit,*
> *all glory and honor is yours, for ever and ever.*

These words themselves have roots in Scripture. They come

in part from St. Paul's letter to the Romans: "For from him and through him and to him are all things. To him be glory for ever. Amen" (Rom 11:36). St. Paul also refers to "the unity of the Spirit" in Ephesians 4:3. Here, the liturgy expresses the Trinitarian nature of our worship in the Mass. We praise the almighty Father best by offering our lives through, with, and in the Son who surrendered Himself completely on Calvary and in the unity of his Spirit who abides in us.

After hearing the priest acclaim that all honor and glory is God's for ever and ever, we respond like the angels, eager to join in this praise of God. We cry out "Amen!" And this is no ordinary "Amen." In it, we join all the great heroes in salvation history—the Levites, Ezra, St. Paul, and all the angels and saints in heaven—in this chorus of unending praise. No wonder St. Jerome said that this Amen in the Mass of the early Christians in Rome "resounded in heaven, as a celestial thunderclap."[84]

---

[84] As cited in Charles Belmonte, 163. In addition to affirming that all honor and glory is God's, the people's "Amen" is an affirmation of the entire Eucharistic prayer. The priest has been representing the Church throughout this prayer. Now the people give their "yes!" to all that the priest has been praying. Accordingly, St. Augustine described this great "Amen" as the people's signature under the prayer of the priest.

# C. The Communion Rite

Now is the time for the final preparations. The bread and wine have been consecrated. The words of institution have been spoken. Our Lord is now truly present before us. In just a few moments, we will receive Jesus' body and blood in holy communion. This next part of the Mass—which includes the Lord's Prayer, the Rite of Peace, the *Agnus Dei,* and other preparatory rites—is meant to lead the people to the sacred point of holy communion and help ensure they are properly disposed to receive the body and blood of Christ.

# 21. The Lord's Prayer

*"Our Father,*
*Who art in heaven,*
*Hallowed be thy name.*
*Thy kingdom come,*
*Thy will be done on earth as it is in heaven.*
*Give us this day our daily bread,*
*And forgive us our trespasses*
*As we forgive those who trespass against us.*
*Lead us not into temptation*
*and deliver us from evil. Amen."*

The Lord's Prayer was taught by Jesus in the gospels (Mt 6:9-13; Lk 11:1-4) and has been used in the Mass throughout the centuries. For some of us, this might be a routine prayer that we learned from childhood and simply repeat every Sunday. Yet it should not be taken for granted. Before we approach the Lord's Prayer, the priest notes what a privilege it is for us to be able to talk to God in this way.

> *"At the Savior's command and formed by divine teaching,*
> *we dare to say..."*

Perhaps the most striking aspect of the Lord's Prayer is how it leads us to address God as "Father." The ancient Jews certainly viewed God as the father of the people of Israel. But it was not at all common for an individual to address God as "Father." Nevertheless, this is precisely what Jesus calls us to do. He taught this prayer to his disciples in the gospels (Mt 6:9-13; Lk 11:1-4), and if he was speaking his native Aramaic, he probably used the word "Abba" for father. This was an intimate, affectionate term similar to "Daddy" (see Mk 14:36; Rom 8:15; Gal 4:4-6). This underscores the intimate relationship we now have with God because of Jesus' work of salvation. Through our union in Christ, God has truly become our Father. We have become "sons in the Son." The profundity of this relationship we sinful creatures have with God is expressed in the opening line of this prayer. The One "who [is] in heaven"—the Almighty, Eternal God—is our Father.

The word *Our* in this prayer also is significant. It points to the deep unity we have together by virtue of our common heavenly Father. All who are united in Christ are truly brothers and sisters in him. In Christ, Jesus' Father has become our Father and we all are the Father's children in the covenant family of God.

The Our Father has traditionally been divided into seven petitions with the first three focused on God (*thy* name, *thy* kingdom, *thy* will) and the last four focused on our needs (give *us*, forgive *us*, lead *us*, deliver *us*).

*Hallowed be thy name:* In the Bible, God's name was associated with God Himself (Gn 32:28-29; Ex 3:14-15; Is 52:6). This petition prays that God's name may be hallowed: that God and his name may be recognized and treated as holy.

*Thy kingdom come:* The prophets foretold how God would restore the Kingdom to Israel and that God Himself would reign over all nations (Is 40:9-11; 52:7-10; Zec 14:9, 16-17). This petition prays that God's reign will be accepted throughout the world in all peoples' hearts, beginning with our own.

*Thy will be done on earth as it is in heaven:* This petition is related to the first two. In heaven, God's will is obeyed perfectly. His name is hallowed and his reign is welcomed by all the angels and saints. We now pray that all on earth may worship God and obey his will in the same way.

*Give us this day our daily bread:* As we saw earlier, in the Bible, bread is the most basic kind of food and was viewed as necessary to sustain life. Mention of bread did not bring to mind simply food or nourishment; it often was also a symbol for support for life in general. The mention of "daily bread" in this petition refers to our daily needs. In particular, it recalls the daily manna given to sustain Israel in the desert (Ex 16:16-22). Just as God gave each person exactly the amount of heavenly bread they needed each day, so he continues to provide for our needs each day today. Finally, this petition also has Eucharistic overtones as the prayer for daily bread points to the Bread of Life we are about to receive in holy communion.

*Forgive us our trespasses as we forgive those who trespass against us:* Before receiving holy communion, we ask God to forgive our sins—to purify us so that we might be holy tabernacles for Jesus who will soon dwell within us. But God's mercy cannot penetrate our hearts as long as we have not forgiven those who have hurt us.[85] Jesus taught that we will receive God's mercy to the extent that we show mercy to others (see Mt 6:14-15; 18:23-35). In the Sermon on the Mount, Jesus even said that before someone approaches the altar to worship God, he should be reconciled with his brother first, if his brother has sinned against him (see Mt 5:23-24). Similarly, before we approach the altar to receive holy communion, we are challenged in this prayer to forgive those who have sinned against us and to be reconciled with our brethren.

*Lead us not into temptation:* This petition is not so much a prayer to avoid all trials and temptations in life. The biblical words express a request that God not allow us to *enter into* temptation in

---

[85] CCC 2840.

the sense of *giving in* to it. It is a prayer that God would strengthen us to overcome the temptations we face. Pope Benedict XVI taught that in this petition, it is as if we are saying to God, "I know that I need trials so that my nature can be purified. When you decide to send me those trials…then please remember that my strength goes only so far. Don't overestimate my capacity. Don't set too wide the boundaries within which I may be tempted, and be close to me with your protecting hand when it becomes too much for me."[86] As St. Paul said, "God is faithful, and he will not let you be tempted beyond your strength, but with the temptation will also provide the way of escape, that you may be able to endure it" (1 Cor 10:13).

*Deliver us from evil:* When this petition is understood from a biblical perspective, we see that we are not praying for deliverance from harm or misfortune in general. In Scripture, the word here for "evil" can be translated "the Evil One." This reminds us that evil is not something abstract. It is not random bad things that happen in the world. In this petition, evil refers to a person—Satan, the fallen angel who opposes God's will and leads others to join him in his rebellion.[87] In this concluding petition, therefore, we are asking that the Father deliver us from Satan, from all his lies, works, and entrapments.

## A New Kind of Peace

> "Deliver us, Lord, we pray, from every evil,
> graciously grant peace in our days,
> that, by the help of your mercy,
> we may be always free from sin
> and safe from all distress,
> as we await the blessed hope
> and the coming of our Savior, Jesus Christ."

Here, we arrive at a prayer that elaborates on the last petition

---

[86] Pope Benedict XVI, *Jesus of Nazareth* (New York: Doubleday, 2007), p. 163.
[87] See CCC, 2851-4.

of the Lord's Prayer: "And deliver us from evil." The priest says, "Deliver us, Lord, we pray, from every evil, graciously grant peace in our days…" The peace envisioned here is more than an absence of war or hostility in the world. The biblical understanding of peace (*shalom*) is first and foremost something profoundly personal and spiritual. It denotes an inner wholeness or well-being that is a gift from God flowing from faithfulness to God's covenant. When individuals entrust their lives to the Lord and follow his plan, they discover a deep inner peace within themselves, and it is this inner peace that flows into the world through right-ordered, harmonious relationships with others.

That this is the kind of peace we pray for in the Mass becomes clear in the next petition. The priest asks the Lord to free us from sin and distress—two things that plague the human condition and cause us to lose our peace. God's law is the pathway to happiness, and breaking it leads to a loss of peace. If we give in to selfishness, pride, envy, lust, or greed, we will never be happy. We will always be insecure, restlessly seeking more control, more attention, more wealth, or more pleasure, while being constantly worried about losing what we already posses.

Christians can experience fears in life that may cause their hearts to lose the peace of God. We might be anxious about a situation at work, at the parish, or in our families. We might be afraid of the future or afraid of suffering. We might be worried about a big decision, about our finances, or about what someone thinks of us. Christians, of course, should give attention to our human responsibilities. But when preoccupations dominate our hearts and cause us to lose our peace, it is a sign that something is wrong spiritually. We are not truly trusting God with our lives.

At this moment in the Mass, the priest prays that Jesus deliver us from all these anxieties that keep us from experiencing the deep peace he wants to give us. And he points out that we make this prayer as we stand between the experience of our trials of this world and the confident expectation of the Lord's coming when he will set all things right. To express this hope, the Liturgy borrows language from Paul's letter to Titus: "as we await the blessed hope and the coming of our Savior, Jesus Christ" (compare Titus 2:13).

### For the Kingdom, the Power and the Glory...

Like the angels in heaven once again, the people respond to the priest's prayer by praising God:

> *"For the kingdom, the power and the glory are yours now and forever."*

This prayer is sometimes known as the Protestant ending of the Lord's Prayer. Though it is not a part of the prayer that Jesus actually taught us (and fittingly is not included in the Our Father recited in the Catholic liturgy) (see Mt 6:9-13; Lk 11:1-4), this prayer does have biblical roots and finds an appropriate home at this moment in the Mass. On a basic level, the prayer reflects similar acclamations found in the heavenly liturgy (Rv 5:12; 19:1). And when we pray it, we come in contact with the Mass of some of the earliest Christians. For these words are taken from a prayer of thanksgiving used in the celebration of the Eucharist in the first generation of Christianity after the apostles.[88]

Moreover, the words themselves reach 1,000 years further back into the Old Testament period. They are derived from King David's climactic praise of God at the end of his reign, representing one of David's last acts as king before he passed the throne on to his son Solomon:

> "Blessed art thou, O Lord, the God of Israel our father,
> for ever and ever. Thine, O Lord, is the greatness, and
> *the power, and the glory*, and the victory, and the maj-
> esty; for all that is in the heavens and in the earth is

---

[88] See *Didache* (c. A.D. 110), 10.

thine; *thine is the kingdom*, O Lord, and thou art exalted
as head above all" (1 Chr 29:10-11).

David was the most famous of all the kings. He was the powerful and glorious monarch whose kingdom brought Israel to one of its highest points in its history. And yet, at the end of his reign, David humbly recognizes that all the good that came through his kingship came from God. All the power, glory and kingdom he possessed was not his own, but God's. David says, "Thine, O Lord, is the greatness, and the power and the glory...thine is the kingdom."

At every Mass, we echo these words of King David. In doing so, we acknowledge God as the Lord of our lives and praise him for all the blessings he bestows upon us. Whatever good we might do, whatever success we might experience, ultimately comes from God: "For the kingdom, the power and the glory are *yours* now and forever."

# 22. The Rite of Peace

*"Lord Jesus Christ,*
*who said to your apostles,*
*Peace I leave you, my peace I give you,*
*look not on our sins,*
*but on the faith of your Church,*
*and graciously grant her peace and unity*
*in accordance with your will..."*

After petitioning the Father for the gift of peace, the priest now addresses Jesus, recalling his words to the apostles at the Last Supper: "Peace I leave with you; my peace I give to you" (Jn 14:27). In this verse, Jesus goes on to explain that the kind of peace he offers is "not as the world gives."

Many people seek the security and peace of this world, which is a peace based on success, on everything going well, on avoiding problems and suffering. But this kind of peace is quite fragile and fleeting. It is dependent on external circumstances that can easily change (one's health, one's job, one's financial situation, how one is viewed by others). To base one's life on these shaky foundations does not bring real peace at all. It breeds insecurity.

Christ, however, offers us a deeper, longer lasting peace—one that the world does not give. When we allow Jesus to be the foundation of our lives and live according to his plan for us, he gives us an internal, spiritual peace that can withstand life's many disappointments, trials, and sufferings. This is the kind of peace of heart that also builds true unity within marriages, families, communities, parishes, and nations. And this is what the priest prays for at this moment in the liturgy. He then turns toward the people, and addresses them with words of peace that recall St. Paul's greeting of peace found at in many of his letters (see Rom 1:7; 1 Cor 1:3; Gal 1:3): "The peace of the Lord be with you always."

## The Sign of Peace

Next comes the sign of peace, which reflects ancient Christian practice and the exhortations of Saints Peter and Paul: "Greet one another with a holy kiss" (Rom 16:16; 1 Cor 16:20; 2 Cor 13:12; see also 1 Thess 5:26; 1 Pet 5:14). The "holy kiss" expressed the fellowship in charity that the early Christians shared and fittingly found its way into the liturgy. As early as the year 155, Justin Martyr mentioned the exchange of the kiss in the Mass. Tertullian, in about A.D. 200, referred to the ritual as a seal on prayer.

In the Mass today, we exchange some sign that expresses peace, communion, and charity. The sign may vary, depending on local custom. In some settings, it might involve shaking hands. In others, it might entail bowing one's head or some other sign.

Whatever the gesture, the rite of peace can be seen as connecting the Our Father with the reception of holy communion about to take place. On one hand, it serves as a beautiful ritual enactment of the Lord's Prayer, which, as we have seen, expresses the unity of all God's children. We call on God not individualistically, separated from each other, but together as brothers and sisters in God's covenant family, saying, "*Our* Father who art in heaven..." Now, the sign of peace expresses this unity in ritual. On the other hand, the sign of peace symbolically anticipates the profound unity the people will share with each other when they receive holy communion.

# 23. *Agnus Dei:* The Fraction, Commingling, and the "Lamb of God"

This part of the Mass includes three rituals we will now consider: the breaking of bread, the commingling of the Body and Blood of Christ, and the recitation of the "Lamb of God" prayer. Here, the priest breaks the Eucharistic host in a symbolic action known as the *fraction* or the breaking of bread. For the ancient Jews, the expression "the breaking of bread" denoted a ritual at the start of a meal in which the head of the home took bread, recited a blessing, and then broke the bread and shared it with those present. The expression took on great importance for the early Christians who associated it with the Eucharist.

The gospels report four occasions when Jesus himself broke bread. The first two take place in two accounts in which he miraculously multiplied loaves to feed large crowds (see Mt 14:19; 15:36; Mk 6:41; 8:6; Lk 9:16). Matthew's gospel in particular helps us to see how this miracle of multiplying loaves foreshadows the Eucharist. When feeding the crowds, Jesus *took* loaves of bread, *blessed* them, *broke* them, and *gave* them to the disciples to distribute to the multitudes (Mt 14:19). Matthew later uses these same four verbs when narrating the institution of the Eucharist at the Last Supper—the third occasion when Jesus broke bread (Mt

26:26; see Mk 14:22; Lk 22:19; 1 Cor 11:24). "Jesus *took* bread, and *blessed*, and *broke* it and *gave* it to the disciples and said…" (Mt 26:26). With these verbal connections, Matthew underscores how the multiplication of loaves prefigures the even greater miracle of the Eucharist. In the former passage, Jesus multiplied loaves to feed a large crowd. In the latter, he offers a supernatural bread, the Eucharistic Bread of Life, to nourish an even greater amount of people, the great multitude of Christians who receive communion throughout the world and throughout the ages.

The fourth instance in which Jesus is reported to have broken bread is in another scene with Eucharistic overtones: the Easter account of Jesus appearing to the two disciples on the road to Emmaus. At first, they did not know it was Jesus who was walking with them, but they recognized him when he "took the bread and blessed, and broke it, and gave it to them" (Lk 24:30).

### Breaking Bread in the Early Church

The Acts of the Apostles describes how the early Church gathered for the breaking of bread—a term which we have already seen was associated with the Eucharist in the gospels and in the letters of Paul. Long before the building of churches, basilicas, and cathedrals, the very first Christians in Jerusalem worshiped God by attending the Temple together and gathering for the breaking of bread in their homes (Acts 2:46). Similarly, years later and far from Jerusalem, the Christians following St. Paul in Troas gathered with him on the first day of the week "to break bread" (Acts 20:7, 11). So important was the gathering for "the breaking of bread" that Acts lists it as one of the four chief characteristics of the lives of the first Christians, alongside devotion to the apostles' teachings, prayer, and fellowship (Acts 2:42).

St Paul himself not only used the expression of breaking bread to describe the Eucharist. He also saw rich symbolism in the ritual of many people partaking of the same loaf of bread. For Paul, this points to the deep unity Christians share when we partake of the one Body of Christ: "The bread which we break, is it not a participation in the body of Christ? Because there is one bread, we who are many are one body, for we all partake of the one bread" (1 Cor 10:16-17). Therefore, when the priest breaks the Eucharistic host in the Mass, the ritual brings to mind this grand tradition of breaking bread—from the Old Testament Jews, to Jesus' practice, to the Apostles and the early Church, down to the present day.

**Commingling:** After breaking the host, the priest places a small piece into the chalice while quietly saying, "May this mingling of the Body and Blood of our Lord Jesus Christ bring eternal life to us who receive it."

This ritual, known as the *commingling*, was used at one time to express the unity of the Church. In Rome, the pope had a small particle of the consecrated host called the *fermentum* (leaven) sent to priests in the city, who placed it in their chalices as a sign of their union with the bishop of Rome. Some also have interpreted this ritual as a symbol reenacting Christ's resurrection. In this view, which has roots in eighth-century Syria, the separate consecrations of the bread and wine in the Mass symbolize the separation of Christ's body and blood in his death, whereas the commingling rite expresses the reunion of Christ's body and blood in his resurrection.

**The Agnus Dei:** While the priest performs the rite of breaking the host and the commingling, the people sing or say the following prayer, known as the *Agnus Dei* (Latin for "Lamb of God"):

> *"Lamb of God, you take away the sins of the world,*
>    *have mercy on us.*
> *Lamb of God, you take away the sins of the world,*
>    *have mercy on us.*
> *Lamb of God, you take away the sins of the world,*
>    *grant us peace."*

The "Lamb of God" is another prayer that takes us right up to God's throne. When we recite these words, we join the myriad of angels who worship Jesus as the victorious Lamb in the heavenly liturgy that St. John describes in the book of Revelation: "Then I looked, and I heard around the throne and the living creatures and the elders the voice of many angels, numbering myriads of myriads and thousands of thousands, saying with a loud voice, 'Worthy is the Lamb who was slain'" (Rv 5:11-12). St. John also saw all creatures worshiping the Lamb: "And I heard every creature in heaven and on earth and under the earth and in the sea, and all therein, saying, 'To him who sits upon the throne and to the Lamb be blessing and honor and glory and might for ever and ever!'" (Rv 5:13). We join this chorus of heaven and earth in worshiping the Lamb when we recite the *Agnus Dei* in the Mass.

It is fitting that we address Jesus, saying "Lamb of God, you take away the sins of the world," for the New Testament reveals Jesus as the new Passover lamb who was sacrificed for our sake. St. Paul calls Jesus "our paschal lamb" who "has been sacrificed" (1 Cor 5:7). The book of Revelation refers to Jesus as the Lamb who was slain (Rv 5:6, 12; 13:8), whose blood washes the garments of the saints (Rv 7:14), and conquers even Satan (Rv 12:11).

John's gospel, in particular, highlights how Jesus, in his death on the cross, should be seen as the Passover lamb sacrificed on our behalf. When John gives the account of the soldiers raising up to Jesus' mouth a sponge of vinegar, he notes it was put on a hyssop branch. Why does John mention this small detail? Because this was the same kind of branch used in the first Passover in Egypt. Moses instructed the elders of Israel to sacrifice the Passover lamb, dip hyssop in the blood of the lamb and use the stained hyssop to mark their doorposts with the lamb's blood (Ex 12:22). John notes this so that we can see Jesus' death as a Passover sacrifice. Just as hyssop was used in the first Passover sacrifice, now it is used on Calvary with Jesus, the new sacrificial Lamb.

In another link with the Passover lamb, John's gospel notes that when the soldiers took Jesus down from the cross, they did not break his legs as was ordinarily done to ensure that the person was truly dead (Jn 19:33). John points this out because the Passover lamb was supposed to be one whose bones were not broken (Ex 12:46). Once again, Jesus' death is portrayed as the sacrifice of a Passover lamb.

## Behold, the Lamb of God

The words of the Lamb of God prayer, however, come most directly from John the Baptist. John is the first person to refer to Jesus as "Lamb of God" (Jn 1:29, 36). When he first saw Jesus during his baptism ministry at the Jordan, he cries out "Behold, the Lamb of God, who takes away the sin of the world!" (Jn 1:29).

There is a lot packed in this short statement. With these words, John is recognizing Jesus as the great Suffering Servant prophesied by Isaiah. Isaiah foretold that God one day would send someone to rescue Israel from sin, and he would do it by suffering "like a lamb that is led to the slaughter" (Is 53:7). Moreover, this servant of the Lord would bear the people's iniquities and "make himself an offering for sin" (Is 53:10-11). And his self-offering would have redemptive power. Through his sacrifice, many will be made righteous (Is 53:11). The mention of a lamb being sacrificed would, of course, bring to mind the Passover lambs. But the new element introduced in Isaiah is the notion of an individual person offering his life as a sacrifice for sin. When John the Baptist calls Jesus the Lamb "who takes away the sin of the world," therefore, he identifies him not only as the Passover lamb, but also as the long-awaited suffering servant of Isaiah 53—the Lamb who would offer his life as a sacrifice for sin.

How fitting it is that we recite the Lamb of God at this precise moment in the Mass! While the priest breaks the host, the people join John the Baptist in recognizing Jesus as the Servant-Lamb of Isaiah 53 who offers his life as a sacrifice for sin. Jesus is the lamb that was led to the slaughter. Jesus is the one whose sacrifice made many righteous. We thus call Jesus "Lamb of God" and say to him that through his death, "you take away the sins of the world."

This prayer is typically repeated three times: "Lamb of God, you take away the sins of the world…" This echoes other prayers repeated three times in the Mass. In the *Confiteor*, we each admitted our guilt three times, saying, "Through my fault, through my fault, through my most grievous fault." Then in the *Kyrie*, we three times cried out for God's mercy. Now, after acclaiming the thrice-holy Lord in the *Sanctus* and just before receiving communion, we ask for mercy and peace from the only one who can free us from our sins—the "Lamb of God" who offered his life for our sake and thus took "away the sins of the world."

One last note: The *Agnus Dei* also includes the repeated plea, "have mercy on us," similar to the *Kyrie*. The last time Jesus is addressed as "Lamb of God," the cry for mercy is changed to a petition for peace. This links the *Agnus Dei* to the sign of peace just given and anticipates the unity that will be forged in receiving the Eucharist.

# 24. Holy Communion

Have you ever thought of the Mass as a wedding feast? When thinking of the Mass, the words "liturgy," "communion," "real presence," or "sacrifice" may easily come to mind. But *a marriage*? Yet from the Church Fathers to the mystical poetry of St. John of the Cross to the theological writings of Pope John Paul II, the Catholic tradition has often described holy communion—the culmination of the Liturgy—as an intimate union with our divine Bridegroom, Jesus, in the Eucharist.

We can understand how the Mass is a wedding feast by considering the words of the priest shortly before we receive communion:

> *"Behold the Lamb of God,*
> *behold him who takes away the sins of the world.*
> *Blessed are those called to the supper of the Lamb."*

These words are taken from a climactic moment in the book of Revelation and indeed, the entire Bible (Rv 19:9). To understand the full force of these words, we need to step back and consider how they appear in the wider context of this part of the book of Revelation.

## "Hallelujah!"

In Revelation 19:1-6, we find the multitudes in heaven along with the angels and elders singing a new song to the Lord. Four times they shout out "Hallelujah!" in their praise of God. This is significant because the important liturgical word "Hallelujah" (which means "praise Yahweh"), while found many times in the Old Testament, is used only four times in the entire New Testament. And all four instances occur right here in rapid fire succession in these six verses from Revelation 19.

This sudden chorus of "Hallelujah's" in Revelation 19:1-6 would bring to mind the famous "Hallel Psalms" of the Old Testament (Psalms 113-118). This group of Psalms are called "Hallel" because a number of them begin or end with "Hallelujah's," praising God for his works of redemption. What is interesting is that these Hallel Psalms were the songs which the Jews would sing during the Passover meal. They sang "Hallelujah" in praise of Yahweh who rescued Israel from the Egyptians in the Exodus and who would redeem his people once again. In fact, these are the very songs which Jesus would have sung during his final Passover meal, the Last Supper, when he instituted the Eucharist (see Mt 26:30; Mk 14:26).

### The Wedding Supper of the Lamb

This background may provide an important clue for understanding the last of the four "Hallelujah's" in Revelation 19 which comes in verse 6—a turning point in the heavenly liturgy when the great multitude resounds in praise of God for the supper of the Lamb:

> *"Hallelujah! For the Lord our God the Almighty reigns.*
> *Let us rejoice and exult and give him the glory,*

---

Note: Portions of this chapter are adapted from an article by the author that appeared in *Lay Witness* magazine. See Edward Sri, "Here Come the Bride ... and the Lamb," *Lay Witness*, October 2000, pp. 6-8.

*for the marriage of the Lamb has come*
*and his Bride has made herself ready." (Rv 19:6-7)*

And the angel instructs John to write: "Blessed are those who are invited to *the marriage supper of the Lamb*" (Rv 19:9).

What is this festive supper of the Lamb? It is the Lord's Supper, the Eucharist. First of all, the *supper* and the *Lamb* bring to mind the Passover supper in which Jews would sacrifice a lamb and eat of it as the main course of the meal. Further, when we read about a Lamb's supper within the chorus of Hallel Psalm-like Hallelujah's in verses 1-6, the Passover allusions become even more evident. Thus, this climactic supper of the Lamb is clearly some type of Passover meal, and in light of the liturgical framework of the book of Revelation, it would be understood as the new Passover of the Eucharist.

But this passage tells us something even more dramatic. In Revelation 19:6-9, the Lamb is revealed to be a bridegroom! And that means this Passover supper is a wedding feast. The Bridegroom-Lamb is Jesus, and the Bride represents us, the Church, whom Jesus is coming to wed. Indeed, this is the wedding feast in which the Lamb unites Himself to his Bride, symbolizing the final consummation of the union between Christ and his Church (see Rv 21-22; Eph 5:21-33). It is in this heavenly marriage between Jesus and the Church that we participate through the Eucharistic liturgy here on earth as a foretaste of the communion we hope to have with our divine bridegroom for all eternity. Therefore, when the priest says, "Blessed are those who are called to the supper of the Lamb," he echoes the angel's invitation to the wedding supper of the Lamb in the Apocalypse (Rv 19:9).

When you hear those words at Mass, do you realize that you are receiving a wedding invitation? You are being called to participate in the marriage feast of Jesus and his Church. And most of all, you are no ordinary guest at this wedding. You are the bride! When you walk down the aisle to receive holy communion, as a member of the Church, you are coming to be united to your bridegroom, Jesus.

Indeed, holy communion has a marital dimension. Husbands and wives give themselves to each other in the marital act, uniting their bodies in the most intimate way possible. Similarly, our divine Bridegroom comes to unite Himself to us in the most intimate way possible here on earth, giving his very body and blood to us in the Eucharist. This is why the tradition of thanksgiving after communion is so important. We should want to rest with Our Lord, to talk to him and thank him at many points in our lives, but most especially as he is dwelling within our souls in those moments after holy communion. No good husband would run off to check email or cut the grass immediately after having intimate relations with his wife. And we should not be so eager to race out of the parking lot, talk to friends or get coffee and doughnuts as our Bridegroom is intimately dwelling within us. This is the time for us to take a few moments to rest with our Beloved, to give him our tender attention and thanksgiving, and to express our love for him.

In this light, the Mass really is a wedding feast. Like a bride who longs to be one with her groom, so our hearts should be filled with ardent longing for holy communion with our divine Bridegroom, whose very Eucharistic body sacramentally enters into ours in the most intimate way possible.

## Lord, I am not worthy

But how can we mere human beings—and sinful ones at that!—dare to approach the all-holy, almighty God in this way? In response to the invitation to the marriage supper of the Eucharist, we say a prayer that on one hand, acknowledges our complete unworthiness to receive our Lord, and at the same time, expresses confidence that Jesus calls us and can heal us:

> *"Lord, I am not worthy*
> *that you should enter under my roof,*
> *but only say the word*
> *and my soul shall be healed."*

These words reflect the humility and trust of the Roman centurion who asked Jesus to heal his servant who is at his house, paralyzed and in distress. As a Gentile outside of God's covenant, and as a Roman officer in charge of one hundred soldiers who were oppressing God's people, this centurion humbly acknowledges that he is not worthy to have Jesus come to his home. Yet he expresses a great faith that surpasses many others in the gospels and amazes even Jesus: He believes Jesus can heal from afar, simply by speaking his word: "But only say the word, and my servant shall be healed" (Mt 8:8). Jesus praises this man for his faith.

Like the centurion, we recognize our unworthiness to have Jesus come under the "roof" of our souls in holy communion. Yet just as the centurion believed Jesus was able to heal his servant, so do we trust that Jesus can heal us as he becomes the most intimate guest of our soul in the Eucharist.

## Mary's First Communion

In a closing reflection on those sacred moments of holy communion, let us turn to John Paul II, who once pondered what it would have been like for Mary to receive the Eucharist for the first time.

First, John Paul II noted a profound connection between Mary carrying Jesus in her womb and the person receiving communion. In a sense, we become like Mary every time we receive the Eucharist. "Mary lived her *Eucharistic faith* even before the institution of the Eucharist, by the very fact that *she offered her virginal womb for the Incarnation of God's Word.*" For nine months, Mary had the body and blood of Jesus within her. At Mass, we receive the sacramental Body and Blood of our Lord. "At the Annunciation, Mary conceived the Son of God in the physical reality of his body and blood, thus anticipating within herself what to some degree happens sacramentally in every believer who receives, under the signs of bread and wine, the Lord's body and blood."[89]

Second, John Paul II pondered how Mary would have felt when she first heard about the Eucharist. She was not present at the Last Supper and presumably would have learned about what happened there from the apostles:

> What must Mary have felt as she heard from the mouth of Peter, John, James and the other Apostles the words spoken at the Last Supper: 'This is my body which is given for you' (Lk 22:19)? The body given up for us and made present under sacramental signs was the same body which she had conceived in her womb![90]

John Paul then beautifully drew out the unique meaning Holy Communion would have had for the Blessed Virgin: "For Mary, receiving the Eucharist must have somehow meant welcoming once more into her womb that heart which had beat in unison with hers..."[91]

What a profound insight! Imagine Mary preparing herself to be reunited with her Son in this way. Imagine the loving attention she gave to Jesus in every holy communion. What a joy it must have been for her to have her Son dwelling within her again! May Mary be a model for us in the way we receive the Eucharist. Let us pray that we may ardently welcome Jesus in every holy communion as Mary received her Son. May the Eucharist cause our hearts to beat ever more in unison with Christ's as Mary's heart beat perfectly with his.

After the distribution of the Eucharist, the priest cleanses the vessels and says the "Prayer after Communion," in which he prays for the spiritual fruits of the Eucharist to take effect in our lives.

---

[89]  John Paul II, *Ecclesia de Eucharistia*, no. 55.

[90]  Ibid., no. 56.

[91]  Ibid., no. 56.

Part V

# The Concluding Rites

# 25. Greeting, Blessing, and Dismissal

*Priest:* Go forth, the Mass is ended.
*People:* Thanks be to God.

The people stand for the closing rites of the Mass, which mirror how the Mass began—with the words "The Lord be with you" and the sign of the cross. This time, the sign of the cross is made while the priest blesses the people in the name of the Father, the Son, and the Holy Spirit.

In the ancient world, it was customary to close an assembly with a formal dismissal. The early Christians felt the need to incorporate a similar conclusion to their liturgical assembly. From the fourth century onward, the Latin words *Ite Missa est* were employed for this task. Literally meaning "Go, you are dismissed," these words are rendered in the new translation of the Mass, "Go forth, the Mass is ended."

What is most significant about this dismissal is that the whole Liturgy receives its name, "the Mass," from the word *Missa* ("dismissal"/"sending") in this closing line. This points to how the Mass ultimately should be seen as a sending forth. As the *Catechism* explains the celebration of the Eucharist is called "Holy Mass" (*Missa*) "because the liturgy in which the mystery of salvation is accomplished concludes with the sending forth (*missio*) of the faithful, so that they may fulfill God's will in their daily lives."[92]

Jesus told the apostles, "As the Father has sent me, even so I send you" (Jn 20:21). The Father sent the Son into the world, to die for our sins and give us a share in his divine life. As we have seen, the entire paschal mystery of Jesus' passion, death and resurrection is made present to us in the Eucharistic liturgy so that we can be more deeply incorporated into Jesus' life and mission. The more deeply the Eucharist unites us to Jesus, the more we will radiate his life and his love in the world around us. The closing line of the liturgy, therefore, is not an aimless dismissal. It is a dismissal with a mission. It is a sending forth of God's people to bring the mysteries of Christ into the world.

---

[92] CCC 1332.

# Index

# About the Author

Edward Sri is provost and professor of theology and Scripture at the Augustine Institute in Denver. In addition, he serves as a visiting professor at Benedictine College in Atchison, Kansas, where he taught full-time for nine years.

Edward is the author of several books, including *The Gospel of Matthew* (Baker Academic), *The Bible Compass: A Catholic's Guide to Navigating the Scriptures* (Ascension Press), *The New Rosary in Scripture: Biblical Insights for Praying the 20 Mysteries* (Servant), *Men, Women, and the Mystery of Love: Practical Insights on John Paul II's Love and Responsibility* (Servant), *Mystery of the Kingdom: On the Gospel of Matthew* (Emmaus Road), *Queen Mother: A Biblical Theology of Mary's Queenship* (Emmaus Road), *Dawn of the Messiah: The Coming of Christ in Scripture* (Servant), and, with Mark Shea, The *Da Vinci Deception: 100 Questions About the Facts and Fiction of* The Da Vinci Code (Ascension Press).

With Curtis Martin, Edward is a founding leader of the Fellowship of Catholic University Students (FOCUS). He regularly appears on EWTN, speaking on Scripture, apologetics, and the Catholic faith. Edward holds a doctorate in sacred theology (S.T.D.) from the Pontifical University of St. Thomas Aquinas in Rome. He resides with his wife, Elizabeth, and their six children in Littleton, Colorado.

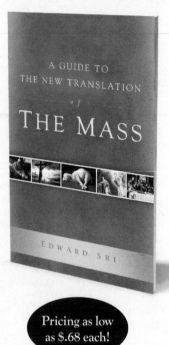

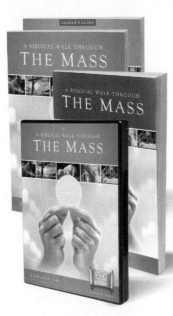